In 1974, the fiftieth anniversary of the publication of *When We Were Very Young*, Christopher Milne published *The Enchanted Places*: a book about his boyhood in Sussex and the experience of being the model for A. A. Milne's Christopher Robin. This was followed by *The Path Through the Trees* in 1979 and *The Hollow on the Hill* in 1982. Of these three books *The Good Book Guide* has written as follows:

'No doubt about it, these books belong with the classics of autobiography – they can be re-read time and again. . . .

'With . . . *The Hollow on the Hill* Milne concludes his trilogy – but what he gives now is an inward journey, a search (as he calls it) for a personal philosophy. To trace his cunning and seemingly tentative thread of thought is best done by each reader. But it is far-ranging, touching down at seminal books and experiences, creeds, and movements, church and laboratory, and much else before its trenchant end. . . . For some, this may even be the one most often turned to of the three.'

' . . . the disarming manner, the element of surprise, and the sudden astringencies keep you reading.' Naomi Lewis *The Observer*

The Hollow
on
the Hill

The search
for a
personal philosophy

by Christopher Milne

with photographs by James Ravilious

Methuen

By the same author

The Enchanted Places
The Path Through the Trees

First published in 1982
by Methuen London Ltd
Copyright © 1982 by Christopher Milne
Photographs copyright © 1982 by James Ravilious
First published in this paperback edition 1983
by Methuen London Ltd
11 New Fetter Lane, London EC4P 4EE

ISBN 0 413 51270 3

Made and printed in Great Britain by
Hazell Watson & Viney Ltd, Aylesbury, Bucks

To A.A.M.
on your hundredth birthday
from C.R.M.
with love

Contents

Preface

In the course of writing this book I was often asked: 'What is it about?' I found this a very hard question to answer. It was much easier to say what it was not about. It was not just more autobiography, continuing the story from where *The Path Through the Trees* had left off. Nor was it about the Devon countryside – although it would be illustrated with photographs of Devon scenery. Yet to confess that it was really about the world, creation and mankind seemed altogether too grandiose a claim to make. Surely one would need to be much more scholarly than I am to write such a book.

Or would one?

An artist can settle down behind his easel and paint whatever he sees. For him a distant field requires no special understanding of glume or palea, no ability to distinguish between meadow fescue and sweet vernal. With a single brush stroke he can say it all. His picture may include trees though he is no arboriculturist, houses though he is no architect, perhaps a bridge or a road though he is no engineer, and in the sky he will add clouds though he knows nothing of meteorology. Yet despite his total ignorance of the detail, he may well be able to tell us something of the landscape in general which the specialist, peering closely, fails to notice.

In the same sort of way – and with the same sort of hope – I have written about science and art, history and religion, evolution and ecology, though I have had no formal training in any of these subjects. I have set up my easel somewhere in outer space with the world spread below me, stretching away to the beginning of time. In what follows I offer, not a finished picture, but a few tentative sketches of some of the more interesting features that have caught my eye. And, like the artist at his easel, I am undeterred by the knowledge that others, more competent than I, have set up their easels at the same spot and produced great masterpieces. I find this not an inhibition but rather a challenge and an encouragement.

Introduction

When I was about six years old someone for some reason gave me a map of Africa. It was a decorative wall map and for many years it decorated the wall in my bedroom.

I loved it. I would stare at it long and frequently. I would follow the Arabs on their camels as they made their way from oasis to oasis. I would join the black men on their hunting expeditions. I would meet crocodiles in the rivers, snakes in the jungles and lions and elephants lurking in the tall grass. All this wealth of adventure and excitement was enclosed within a shape, first seen then, seen many times subsequently, unique and memorable, the shape of Africa. Into this Africa-shape I was to fit all that I later learned about that continent: David Livingstone and Mungo Park, coconuts and pygmies, Gordon and Kitchener, the Pyramids and the Suez Canal. There they belonged in the same sort of way that everything a person is and does and says belongs inside the unique shape of his body.

I suppose that if I had never been given that map I would have visualized 'Africa' in some other way. Perhaps the name alone would have been enough to house my junk-heap of information. Perhaps therefore I can say that my love of maps and my need for them was born then and there on my bedroom wall. For I can visualize nothing on the ground without the help of a map. I cannot enjoy a holiday without a map. I need it to tell me where I am going, what it will be like when I arrive and where I am going next. I need it, no less, to tell me about all the other places I shall not be visiting. Those eighteenth-century road maps that were designed to guide travellers from town to town – ribbons of information chopped into convenient lengths and laid out side by side – I do not consider to be maps at all. They tell you to fork right at the church, but they say nothing about what might happen if instead you forked left. I need a map to tell me all the possibilities, one that shows the whole area.

The whole area? But is any area ever whole? Even an island bounded by the sea has somewhere, near or far, in this direction or that, another island smaller or larger. No map of the Isle of Wight would be complete if it said nothing at all about the mainland of England lying to the north just across the Solent.

The larger the area covered, the smaller the scale and the less the detail. One really needs several maps, starting with a map of the world, perhaps even starting with a map of the solar system. For everything must be seen in relation to its surroundings and even a short journey cannot be fully understood unless one knows what lies over the horizon.

Nor is it just scale that must be decided but also the type of information wanted. You have only to open an atlas to be confronted with maps that show mountains and rivers, maps that distinguish this country from that, maps giving rainfall or population or communication routes or the location of coal mines and oil wells. The possibilities are endless; and so there is no reason why an individual should not draw his own map and claim that it tells him exactly what he wants to know.

But will it be accurate? asks the professional cartographer. Yes and no. It will be accurate in some respects and inaccurate in others. And in this it is in good company, for no map is accurate in all respects, if for no other reason than that you cannot put a curved piece of ground on to a flat piece of paper. And every map must simplify. The map that shows London as a round dot is not implying that London is circular in shape. The map that colours valleys green and mountains brown is not implying that every valley is fertile and every hill top barren. Roads are not in reality red nor rivers blue.

This book is such a map.

There was an area I wished to explore. It was a large area and so it needed a small-scale map. There were ready-made maps to be bought and I bought two or three and found them helpful, but in the end I needed to make my own.

To some extent I have been doing this over most of my life. My early explorations had been very like those early explorations of Africa, landing first on one coast and pushing inland, then landing on another. I once picked up an old atlas for half a crown at an auction and there was Africa with its outline recognizably complete and suitably coloured but in the centre was a white area and across it were written the words, 'Terra Incognita'. The final expeditions had yet to be made, the final surveys yet be carried out.

This book describes what I might call my own final expedition, and it is followed by a complete survey of the entire area set out in what I hope is a logical sequence. In addition I have added a preliminary chapter to describe (very briefly, to avoid repeating myself) the more important discoveries of earlier expeditions. They may have made their mistakes but, as will be seen, they established bases on opposite coasts from which that final assault could be launched.

1 *Early Attempts at Cartography*

Another present, arriving a year or two after my map of Africa, was a terrestrial globe, and that too became a treasured possession. I used to sit in front of it and spin it, sometimes slowly, sometimes fast, and watch the countries of the world go by. What a lot of them were coloured red! Red was British. What a lot of the world belonged to us! What a great and powerful nation we were! This thought made me feel not just how lucky I was to have been born British, but how unlucky the others were to have been born foreign. Indeed I used to feel quite sad for the French and the Spanish and the black men who lived in my beloved Africa.

What my globe told me was confirmed by what I learned elsewhere. At school we were told how Wolfe had beaten Montcalm to capture Canada, how Clive had captured India, how Drake had defeated the Spanish and Nelson the French. History, it seemed, was one long succession of British victories. In the books I read – books by Henty, Kingston and Ballantyne – I learned that Jack and his comrades had only to shout 'Huzzah' for the dagoes to fling up their hands and surrender. And from the placards on hoardings I learned that 'British is Best'. Of course it was! Who could doubt it?

So from an early age my world was divided into a hierarchy with the British at the top, other white men next and coloured people at the bottom.

To this national hierarchy was added, perhaps rather less explicitly, another − a class hierarchy: upper, middle and lower. Again I was lucky. I was upper. And again I felt a twinge of guilt and moments of sadness for those who by misfortune were lower.

Within each hierarchy were barriers keeping their groups apart. I was British. It was impossible for me to cross the barrier and become French; and though I could (and did) paint my face black and stick feathers in my hair, I never became an African or a Red Indian. Class barriers were almost as high. When I was a child I was allowed on occasion to cross them and mix with those below me, but the mixing was controlled and certain proprieties had to be observed. As I grew older these opportunities became fewer.

And there was a third hierarchy, of which I was less conscious because the group to which I belonged was such a vast one that I was scarcely able to see beyond its boundaries to those, less fortunate, on the other side. This was the hierarchy of religion.

Nationality, class and religion: these three determined the sort of life I led − where I lived, who were my companions, what I did and what I thought. At school they formed the three axioms of my life. Nationality: British. Class: upper. Religion: Christian. No one argued the possible superiority of other nations. No one disputed the justness of the social order. No one defended the heathen. There were no Fascists, no socialists and no atheists at any of my schools.

It was when I left school that I began to question all three axioms. Within a few months the war had started. I spent a year at Cambridge and then five years in the army. I could scarcely have had a more rapid or a more thorough introduction to life, to death and to the outside world.

I made my first adult forays across the class barrier in the summer of 1940. I joined the Local Defence Volunteers and shared night duties with the postman, the coalman and the cowman. A year later I crossed again. I joined the Royal Engineers as a sapper and did my recruit training in the company of miners, navvies and bricklayers. In 1942, however, I returned to my own side to become an officer.

In the army of those days the hierarchy of rank almost exactly paralleled the hierarchy of class and the barriers were no less formidable. I found them at their worst soon after I was commissioned. I was posted to a division that almost immediately set sail for the Middle East. On the troopship that carried us round the Cape to the Persian Gulf the officers occupied the cabin accommodation and enjoyed all the comforts that in peacetime had belonged to the passengers. The men were battened down like cargo in the holds.

In Iraq, where we were stationed for four months, it was much the same. There were three other officers in my unit and the four of us lived very comfortably in what – though largely built of mud – could almost be described as a house. The men lived twelve to a tent so small that when they were all lying down no floor space remained. Thus we shared a cold and very wet winter.

I was a platoon commander and had about forty men under me. After morning parade they would be given their tasks for the day – working on various pieces of equipment – and I would go about mine. They worked. I supervised. Across the barrier that separated us I would watch them rather as a zoo superintendent might watch a cage of animals. I was very proud of them and proud to command them. I knew them individually and liked them. Some I liked very much indeed. But they lived in their world and

I lived in mine. Often I would yearn to join them; and very, very occasionally I was able to do so.

Very occasionally we would be given some other task, one that took us away from the company and into the mountains, I and my men. And then it would be as if a sluice were opened and something gushed out from me to join and mingle with something of theirs until the levels were equal and tranquillity came. I never regretted that I was an officer. I much enjoyed the company of my fellow officers. But I needed these periods when the barriers of rank could be breached and it could be once again as it had first been in Sussex on night duty outside the village hall. I was no socialist. I had no wish to destroy the class system or reverse its hierarchy. It was just that I had discovered unsuspected moments of supreme happiness in equality. Thus – unconsciously and passively – I was challenging one of the three axioms of my youth.

At much the same time and in much the same way I began to challenge another of the axioms. In Iraq I met for the first time soldiers of the Indian Army, members not merely of another nation but of another race, yet equal partners with us in the war against Germany. And again I felt this strange surge of fellowship towards them, a feeling that what we had in common was far stronger than what separated us. This feeling recurred when, in the autumn of 1943, we landed in Italy, and this time it was directed towards the Italian civilians – the *contadini* of the south. We were the conquerors and they were a defeated nation. We could march over their land and requisition their property. Yet just occasionally all this could be forgotten, and I could enjoy with an Italian – it might be an old man or a young child – a relationship whose peculiar piquancy sprang from the fact that we were from different nations. This was something that I was to experience more strongly after the war when I returned to Italy year after year on holiday. To be once again among Italians is to feel that I have come home.

This brings me to Christianity.

'God made them, high or lowly, and order'd their estate.' Christ may have preached the equality of man before God, but in the Christian ethic three inequalities are still to be found. The first establishes within the Christian community a pastor/flock relationship which, though it undoubtedly appeals to some, does not appeal to me. The second (to put it very generally) states the superiority of Christianity over other religions and so tends to breed an attitude towards non-Christians not so very different from the attitude I felt as a boy towards foreigners and which I was later to reject – a feeling that I was better than they. The third states the superiority of man over the rest of creation. This may seem beyond question; for who can deny that man is cleverer than the beasts of the field or the flowers that grow under his feet? I am not claiming that dogs have immortal souls or that men are in reality no more intelligent than insects. What I do say is that this God–man–nature hierarchy encourages man to believe that he has the right to dominate the rest of the natural world and bend it to his purpose. As I will argue later, this attitude, once so beneficial to mankind, has now become extremely dangerous.

In my book, *The Path Through the Trees*, I described the two different forms of relationship that an individual can establish with others as either 'end-to-end' or 'side-by-side'. The first is the hierarchical relationship which puts one individual either above or below another. The second is the relationship that exists between equals. I dislike the first. I am unhappy to adopt it myself, as unhappy to command as to be commanded; but even more do I dislike seeing it adopted by others – the Englishman who is aggressively English when he is abroad, the Christian who so patently despises the views of non-Christians, the man who shouts at his dog or bulldozes his way through the countryside. And I so greatly prefer the second in my relationships not only with my fellow men but with all nature. This is not something I express publicly. I am the active champion of no cause. I subscribe to no religious or political organization. It is merely something I am aware of – a feeling of deep happiness when I can ignore all three barriers and join those on the other side and relax in their company.

A love of nature was something I discovered as a child, for we lived in the country and I went to school in the country. Most boys enjoy country life but they do not all enjoy it in the same way. I enjoyed it quietly, contemplatively and usually alone. Once again the war was to teach me something – although the lesson was not to be fully understood until more recently. During the war there were many times when I was very frightened. On such occasions one is like a man flung into a rough sea who clings desperately to anything within reach, or like a frightened child who clings to its mother. Most soldiers clung to each other, that is to say they found courage in the comradeship of their fellows. I did not. I found it instead in the Italian countryside, in nature. Being alone never frightened me, even at night, provided I was in contact with my surroundings – with the grass underfoot, with the dim shapes of trees and distant mountains. This was what I clung to. And if I had worn a talisman round my neck to protect me from danger, a medallion with a picture, the picture would have been not a portrait but a landscape.

I have mentioned these three axioms of my childhood because I think it is important to see that my attitude towards all three was the same. I did not deliberately set myself to act consistently; I was not even aware at the time that I was acting consistently; it is only in retrospect that I find this to have been so. And my conclusion must be that, although the seeds of Christianity were undoubtedly scattered over me as a child and took root and sprang up, they later withered and died at least partly because the soil was unsuitable, inhospitable not just to them but to other seeds requiring similar soil.

But a seed requires more than just the right soil and Christianity demands more from its adherents than passive acceptance. It demands certain beliefs and it welcomes their public expression. As a boy this meant saying my prayers every night and going to school chapel every Sunday. If I enjoyed chapel services it was largely because I enjoyed singing. Perhaps if my tenor voice had been as good as my treble this enjoyment might have continued after the age of fifteen, though I doubt if I would ever have derived much pleasure from army church parades. In one's nightly prayers one comes, almost literally, face to face with one's God; that is to say, it is almost impossible to pray to someone without in some way visualizing that person, giving him some sort of hazy outline, some sort of a face. We talk of God as 'He' rather than 'She' or 'It', and so the outline is vaguely human, the face vaguely masculine. This is entirely acceptable to the child but today may be less acceptable to the adult, even the adult Christian. Round about the age of eighteen it became unacceptable to me. The vision faded. I was reluctant to abandon my prayers and so I searched for a new vision. I abandoned my picture of an external God and directed my prayers instead towards some sort of God within me. I think it very possible that if I had tried to define this God in words I might well have chosen those later used by the American theologian Paul Tillich: 'the ground of my being'. Not long afterwards even this vision faded and I stopped praying altogether. This was somewhere around the beginning of the war. As a soldier I described myself, for convenience if little else, as 'C of E', but within me was a vacuum waiting to be filled.

The filling up process began when I was a lance-corporal stationed at Barton Stacey in Hampshire with quite a lot of spare time for reading and occasional opportunities for visiting Winchester. And so one after-noon found me in a Winchester bookshop. I was looking for something instructive rather than entertaining, some-thing that might perhaps link the world I had left with the world I was entering – the world of mathematics with the world of military engineering. So I made my way to the shelves where they kept the Everyman Library – I had a special fondness for those books – and let my eyes wander along the many titles. And the one that held them was *The Grammar of Science*.

I said earlier that I was to need a map to make sense of my world, that there were ready-made maps to be bought and that I would buy two or three and find them helpful. This was my first.

I bought it and took it back to my hut and – most extraordinarily – I have it still. It is by Karl Pearson, a Mathematical Scholar and Fellow of Kings College, Cam-bridge, and it was first published in 1892. It was a happy choice. This I realized as soon as I began to read; but it was many years before I was to appreciate just how well I had chosen. Quite by chance I had met my John the Baptist.

Very briefly, *The Grammar* can be described as a history of scientific discovery from the earliest times to the end of the nineteenth century (my edition has a later appendix that refers briefly to Einstein's Theory of Relativity). But it is more than just a history of science. It is a philosophy of science and one, moreover, that points towards a philosophy of life. And it was here that I found Pearson at his most enthralling.

At school 'science' had been a disappointment. I had hoped that it might combine the mental pleasures of mathematics with the practical pleasures of doing things with my hands. But in fact it combined only what was tedious: the dull calculations that followed from dull weighings and measurings. I was no scientist. I remained a mathematician. And so, if I was to return to look again at science, a fellow mathematician was for me the best possible guide.

What exactly is the scientist trying to do? How exactly does he set about his task? Before one could contemplate his discoveries one must first understand what Pearson called 'the scientific method' and then one must understand what was meant by a 'scientific law'. After that one could see how this scientific method could be extended into other fields – indeed into all fields of human activity. And so, in Pearson's words, one arrived at 'a creed of life', one which he loved and served 'as men in great religious epochs served the church'.

Thus he preached his gospel of reason . . . and of course I was a ready convert. How could it have been otherwise? Who at my age and in those days did not need a creed of life? In an uncertain world we need certainties to cling to. At that particular time, when the whole of civilization seemed on the point of collapsing around us, when the distant lights of victory, survival and peace were out of sight over the horizon and (as far as I was concerned) not worth bothering about, the one and only certainty in my life was that I was fighting on the side of Good against the Forces of Evil. The certainties of my boyhood, the truths I had been taught and had accepted, were, in the general avalanche, fast crumbling away. I needed a new philosophy to replace them. I needed to look at the world with a fresh eye and a fresh understanding. It would be a stern eye, grim, realistic, unromantic . . . and in *The Grammar* it found what it wanted. Or rather it found, not the ultimate answer, but the road that was to lead there. And since today I still see the world in part through Pearson's eyes, when I begin, later in this book, my own attempts at a complete cartography, his *Grammar* will be my starting point.

If Pearson was my John the Baptist, I was to meet my Christ four years later. I have described the encounter in my book, *The Enchanted Places*. I was in Italy and my father, who used to send me books to read, chose one with extra care and deliberation but, not wishing to influence my reaction to it, sent it without comment. It was Winwood Reade's *The Martyrdom of Man*. I read it and at once all my growing doubts were swept away. I was offered in their place a new vision of the world that I found totally satisfying. The feelings with which I seized on the truth that Reade offered me were indeed the feelings of a convert towards a new-found faith.

My two books, *The Grammar* and *The Martyrdom*, though I had acquired them in two quite different ways, perfectly complemented each other and had the most profound influence on me. I wonder how many others have read them as a pair and been similarly influenced. I wonder, too, what difference it would have made if I had not read them. Though I would have missed the thrill of those sudden blinding flashes of light, that brilliant dawn of understanding, my guess is that daylight – the same daylight – would have come in the end.

Reade and Pearson were near contemporaries. They were born within twenty years of each other and twenty years separated the publication of their two great works. Both were rationalists. Pearson's god was 'reason', Reade's was 'intellect'. Pearson approached his philosophy through a study of science, Reade through a study of history. How different both these subjects were from the 'science' and 'history' I had been taught at school! At school they had been doled out in pre-packed portions for easy assimilation: 'heat, light, sound', 'inorganic chemistry', 'statics and dynamics', 'the Tudors and Stuarts'. I had to wait for Winwood Reade before I could see beyond *The History of England Book 3* to the history of the world – and I found it every bit as enthralling as had been Pearson's history of science.

The map that Reade offered me was necessarily small in scale and no doubt full of omissions and simplifications, but it gave me for the first time a shape that I could contemplate, like the shape of my childhood map of Africa, an outline that was complete. For me the novelty of this new map was that it divided the world into continental regions quite different from anything I might have expected. Two of these were of particular interest because I had already begun my own localized attempts to survey them.

The first was 'war' – and what I shall be saying in a later chapter owes much to what I here read. The second was 'religion'.

Once again I was being shown something in a new way, not packaged as it had been at school into divinity lessons and chapel services. Once again the scale of the map was small and the area covered large. And so for the first time I saw Christianity as something that began, not a mere two thousand years ago, not even a thousand years before that, when Moses led the Children of Israel out of Egypt, but as something whose origin went back to the beginning of man's life on earth. The Christianity I had been taught at school was only a tiny part of this larger whole – the history of religious belief.

Pearson had taught me to look no further than I could see. The scientist's task, he said, was to describe 'how', not to attempt to answer 'why?'; and he fiercely attacked the 'metaphysicians' who speculated about 'first causes'. I was never entirely clear who these metaphysicians were, but I was eager to adopt his scientific attitude towards life and its problems and quick to spot any unscientific arguments offered by others. However, where Pearson had only hinted, Reade was explicit. The metaphysicians who speculated about first causes became the priests who dogmatized about God.

It was as if, lost and alone, I had suddenly come across someone who was going my way and in whose company I could now travel. Never before had I met anyone who was willing to admit he was not a Christian. Never before had I heard arguments against Christian belief that so closely echoed my own.

Leaning over Reade's shoulder and studying his map I could see the great contributions that both war and religion had made to man's progress. I could see how religious beliefs had been born and what benefits they had brought. But the time had now come when rational, intelligent man should reject them – as he should also reject war. I saw that Pearson had already rejected them as quite unacceptable to a scientific view of the world. Together Pearson and Reade gave me the moral courage to admit to myself – if not immediately to others – inner thoughts that had been steadily maturing. I wholeheartedly supported Christian morality and I was well aware of the enormous debt western culture owed to the Christian faith. But central to Christianity were certain beliefs about God, about Christ and about life after death which – like shoes that one is outgrowing – were becoming more and more uncomfortable. I abandoned them, and the relief was enormous.

But Reade's map covered more than just the past: it included the future.

From time to time as we plod on we raise our eyes and look ahead. Where exactly are we going? Most of the time I was happy to think that I might be going home, that one day the war would be over and I could return to England. Yet occasionally one needs a more distant goal, something perhaps so distant that we ourselves in this life will never reach it. Life after death? Heaven? Reade shook his head. No. That was mere illusion. 'Our faith', he wrote, 'is in the perfectability of man.' It was enough for him and it was enough for me.

Thus by the end of the war I could have described myself as a rationalist, an agnostic and a humanist. I had found what I had been seeking. I need look no further. As with those early navigators who crossed the ocean, made landfall and explored the unknown coast, it didn't occur to me that this was only one side of a vast new continent and that there would be another and different coast on the opposite side.

Dare I suggest that, though my two pilots may have been unusual, my voyage from belief to disbelief was a commonplace one. The small child's knowledge of the world outside his immediate surroundings comes to him from the reports of others. These he naturally accepts as true: he has no reason to do otherwise. If I tell a three-year-old that my cat can fly, he will believe me. He knows that birds and fairies and angels fly. So why not cats? But as he grows older he discovers that not all reports are true, and gradually he learns to distinguish between those that are and those that are not, between the likely and the unlikely, between reliable and unreliable sources. Flying cats join fairies. But what about angels? What about the Bible story? At first it is accepted. Later comes the realization that it has every appearance of being yet another fairy story. But however great the impulse to discard it, there are two pressures that make this difficult. The first is public opinion. In a world of universal belief it required a lot of courage to proclaim oneself an unbeliever. The second is fear, the fear that if, after all, one is mistaken, one risks the wrath of God and eternal damnation.

Clearly the more people who have publicly announced their disbelief, the easier it becomes to join them; and so, every generation, more and more young people travel that ever broader and smoother road. The church may regret this, but it should cause no surprise. To link – as so many Christians then proceed to do – orthodox religious belief with orthodox morality only encourages those who have rejected the one to reject the other.

But however content I was with my new philosophy, a puzzle remained. How could it be that though the voice of reason spoke so clearly and unambiguously, so many could fail to hear it? If I was right – and reason insisted that I was – it followed that these others were wrong. It was a puzzle that remained at the back of my mind for many years. Then, in the early 1960s, it came to the front.

It was arranged by our local church that a series of monthly discussion groups would be held in various private houses throughout the parish. Fellow Christians would meet and talk about Christianity. One of these groups was, however, rather different. Host and hostess, wanting a more lively discussion, welcomed all comers; and since they were friends of ours, they welcomed us.

Hitherto I had kept my beliefs largely to myself. If they were for sharing, they were for sharing only with other unbelievers. I had no wish to argue with those who held different views. Now, for the first time, I found myself in a mainly Christian gathering with no option but to argue.

Those early discussions were indeed lively. We were like strange dogs meeting in the road. We tiptoed warily round each other, teeth bared in sudden snarls of self-defence. How heated we got! It was said that the vicar (who usually joined us) lay awake all night, his mind in turmoil.

Was it, I wonder, a coincidence that the ferment of ideas that seethed and bubbled at our monthly meetings was matched by an equal ferment seething and bubbling in the outside world? In 1963 John Robinson, then Bishop of Woolwich, published *Honest to God*. Here was a book to sell in our bookshop. Here was a book for our group to discuss. And, to my enormous surprise, I found myself defending a bishop against the jibes of a curate. For Robinson's God, far removed from the God of traditional belief, was little different from what – if I had needed one – would have been my own.

As a bookseller I soon discovered that *Honest to God* was only the start of what was to become a flood of literature that advanced the boundaries of Christianity and humanism until they were within amicable talking distance of each other. In this flood was one in particular: John Macmurray's *Reason and Emotion*, the third of my ready-made maps.

It was not a new book. It had been first published in 1935. It was, however, newly reissued in paperback to make its contribution to the debate. I cannot remember what drew me to it. It was not, I think, the fact that it carried inside its front cover a recommendation by my great-uncle, Basil de Selincourt. Perhaps it was no more than its title.

Reason and emotion. With Pearson as my mentor I had studied reason and I knew that reason could never lead to Christianity. Pearson had sternly rejected emotion as unworthy of thinking man. Did Macmurray agree? He did not.

I was now reading rather more critically, selecting only

what I needed and rejecting the rest. I selected only two items from Macmurray. The first dealt with the roles of science and religion.

There were, he said, three fields of human experience. The first concerns our relationship with the material world, the world of things. This is the field explored by science. The second concerns our relationship with the world of life. This is the field explored by art. The third concerns our relationship with our fellow men. This is the field explored by religion. So here at last was the answer to my puzzle. Science and religion were operating in different fields and so, provided there was no straying over the borderline, there was no conflict between them. I had confined myself to the scientific field in which there was no place for God. In the religious field, the field of human relationships, there might well be conflicting thoughts on the precise nature of the Deity, but these were for priests to argue about, not scientists.

The second item that I seized upon lay quite simply in the book's title, *Reason and Emotion*. I let the author interpret those words in his own way. A thought had suddenly broken cover in my mind and I set off in pursuit.

Thus it was I came to the opposite side of my continent, the coast of emotion, and landed there and began my exploration. Pearson had said that reason should be our sole guide in all our affairs. I was now disagreeing with him. Man had another guide, one that spoke with equal authority and wisdom: emotion. There were occasions when we should listen to the voice of reason. There were other occasions when the voice of emotion was to be preferred. My task was to distinguish between these occasions, to draw a dividing line between the rational half of my world and the emotional half. Pearson had taught me what was meant by a rational truth. I had to decide what, if anything, was meant by an emotional truth. And finally the distinction I was making in my own reactions to the world around me I had to be able to make in the reactions of others.

I will be saying much more about this in later chapters and I hope making it all a great deal clearer. Let me here just give a small practical application that helped me as a bookseller. We were at that time selling a lot of children's books, especially to school libraries. These fell into two distinct categories, fiction and non-fiction. These two categories, I now saw, almost exactly paralleled the two halves of my world. Factual books explored the rational world, fiction the emotional. In the rational world people behaved like machines. Only in the emotional world did they come alive, loving, hating, fearing, hoping; and so only in his storybooks did a child meet real flesh-and-blood human beings and become familiar with all the inner conflicts that pulled them this way and that. And as he learned to understand others, so he would come nearer to understanding himself. At a time when it seemed to me that schools and parents were paying too little attention to the outstandingly good children's fiction then being written, here was an argument to redress the balance.

I had thus divided my world into its two halves. I had investigated both, and I was content with what I had discovered. My philosophy once again seemed complete and it satisfied me. But I see now that it was only the two coasts that I knew. I had yet to cross from the one to the other and explore the *terra incognita* that lay between them.

The rest of this book describes that expedition and what followed from it. It led to the discovery that reason and emotion were not, as I had supposed, separate but had a common origin that linked them together. It was as if in the hinterland lay a mountain range that dominated the entire country. From its summit I could look down in all directions and see now a continuous coastline. My country had a shape. I could map it and understand it.

One thing only remains to be added. I had thought that I had said all I wanted to say about my religious beliefs in my last book, *The Path Through the Trees*. I had no wish either privately or publicly to re-examine them. And so, when I sat down to begin a third book, it was an altogether different one that I had in mind. It was something much more modest. I was planning to explore and map the small area of Devon hillside where I live with the idea of writing its natural history.

It was while I was lying in a hollow on my hillside with a notebook in my hand one cold, clear day in late April that I chanced on the clue that diverted me into writing an altogether different book.

2   *The Hollow on the Hill*

Imagine, first, a pyramid. Then consider two sides of that pyramid. They are triangular in shape, share a common edge and have a common apex. This is very roughly the shape of our piece of land at Embridge. If you extend the base of one of the triangles in both directions, you have the valley that runs down to the sea; and if you extend backwards the base of the other triangle, this gives you the second valley that runs into the first. Here in the second valley at the base of the second triangle is our house.

The two triangles are unequal, having different slopes. The first (which if you view it from the top is on the left) rises gently – one in four; the second much more steeply – one in two. As might be expected, the steeper side is the rockier. It was here that they came – our predecessors – to get stone for their walls; and in two places you can see where they dug. The rock is never far beneath the surface. The earth that covers it is dark, almost black, like peat, a compost of oak leaves and bracken. In winter it looks rich and fertile but in the summer it dries almost to dust; and water, unable to penetrate, rolls off its surface. Dig a few inches and you come to stones. Dig a few inches further and you are into solid rock. It is a slate-like rock that splits readily, and the roots of trees, thrusting downwards in search of moisture, cleave it like so many small wedges. You can see this in the two places where the stone was quarried: the thin skin of earth, the jumble of loose stones and then the strata of rock, broken and crumbling at the top, firm and solid at the bottom. As you flake away at the loose rock so you expose the thread-like roots. The trees too have been quarrying here. Rock is crumbled to stone, stone to dust. Leaves fall and rot and mingle with the dust. Then comes the rain to wash away the surface. After a storm our little river is swollen and brown as it carries its burden of hill earth out to sea. It is a slow process. It will take many millions of years before our slope has been levelled flat. But here, as the seasons go by, you can see the process at work.

On the other triangle, where the slope is gentler, the earth is deeper and paler, light brown in colour, and you can dig down a foot or more without obstruction. It is on this slope that I have planted most of my trees.

There were trees here when we came, trees on both slopes. On the gentler one were apples and hazels; on the steeper one oaks and blackthorn. And on the ridge that linked them stood a giant pine. The pine towered up, gaunt and dying, a threat to all that lay within its range, and so we felled it. Some of the apples were dying too, and one by one as they go we are replacing them with others. Near the top are two that throw such a canopy of shade that they alone turn that part of the hillside into woodland. But it was mainly the blackthorn and brambles that kept the grass at bay and gave us that bare, leafy floor that – almost more than the trees – is the essence of a wood.

Thus on our lower, gentler slope we had what we called our orchard and at the top we had what we called our copse. And clearly the first thing to do was to cut a path up the hillside so that we could get to it.

Of all the many things one can do on one's piece of land, making a path is what I enjoy the most. I like building walls, levelling lawns, putting up fences, scything grass, chopping down old trees, planting new ones; but none of these gives quite the delight of making a path.

Most tools are a pleasure to handle for their own sake. They become an extension of one's body and something of oneself flows down them into their blade. The blade becomes alive and sensitive, and eye and ear and finger are soothed and satisfied as the tool goes about its work – as the axe bites deeper and deeper into the tree, as the grass falls before the scythe, as the flake of wood curls away before the chisel. But pick and spade and mattock, the tools of the path-maker, give me no such delight. They give me only an aching back. So why do I so much enjoy making a path? It is a complicated reason.

A garden path – if it is more than just ten yards of paving linking garden gate to front door – takes for its model the true footpath; and the true footpath is not planned and dug, but is something which has happened over the centuries as generations of feet have agreed that this was the best way of getting to wherever it was they were bound for. It was feet that chose and made the route. Perhaps later a spade may have come along to do a little improving, but this was merely to confirm what the feet had already discovered. So a true footpath fits, comfortably and naturally, into its setting, and our own feet follow it, hardly needing our eyes to guide them.

More than that, footpaths give the traveller reassurance. They *go* somewhere. They are not likely to abandon him in the middle of the unknown. They may traverse difficult or dangerous country but they are in themselves safe, securely anchored at both ends, the lifelines along which men can move without fear. We are never entirely alone on a path. The man who walked there yesterday and whose bootprint shows so clearly in muddy places – he is with us; and so are all the others. All who have ever travelled that way are our companions.

But if man needs a sense of security, he likes it spiced with a little insecurity. We like our safety tinged with risk, and even the most unadventurous is an explorer at heart. So the path that takes us straight to its destination is a dull one indeed. The Romans may have been famous for their roads. But they were engineers, not artists. There is a place for the straight road, certainly, but a straight road carries only the one message and when we have read it we have read it. The winding road, however, is a continuous story. Each bend is a mystery and rounding it a discovery. Paint me a landscape. Make it as beautiful as you can with trees and bushes and distant hills. Yes, I will agree that it is beautiful. But it is static. It exists in space but not in time. Add a footpath and immediately it comes to life. It moves. It has a past and a future. There are people on the path travelling along it, and I am there too. Each corner beckons me. On and on I go . . .

How many hundreds of footpaths have I followed in my wanderings through the countryside? How many thousands of miles have I covered, and how many happy memories accumulated? These are the delights that will be waiting for me when I walk my own footpath; and, as I wield my mattock and hack away at the tussocks of grass comes the added delight of being the architect and engineer of my own happiness.

Thus, blistered and aching, but wearing my blisters proudly like wounds won in battle, I rounded the hillside and came to the first of our apple trees.

Here was a good place to pause and look back down the way I had come and admire my work. So I made a level place beneath the apple tree. I skinned off the turf, then cut into the hillside and threw the earth forward, and finally replaced the turf and tramped it down firm. Here I could sit, lord of all the lands that lay below me, and contemplate my domain. Here I established my base camp, my garrison, and from here I planned my final assault on the summit.

I had rounded the shoulder of the hill, my triangle was narrowing towards its apex and I was now in sight of the top. I could zigzag up the last slope: this would enable me to continue my gentle gradient. But somehow it seemed an artificial thing to do. The natural way was to go straight up, and if this was in places awkwardly steep, then I would have to cut steps.

This I did until at last I was face to face with the wild tangle of bramble and blackthorn that held the summit. Then came the battle – bloody hand-to-hand fighting it was – as I slashed my way forwards against an enemy that fought back savagely.

Blackthorn is unique. It is the only tree growing wild in Britain that is (it seems to me) totally hostile to man. Where all other trees are graceful, blackthorn is not just ugly, it is aggressively ugly, as if to show how little it cares for our sensibilities. It juts and twists and stabs and writhes, its grotesque trunk culminating in a tangled lop-sided head. Other trees may have thorns. Only the blackthorn has one which, once in your flesh, is impossible to remove intact. Dig it up? You cannot, for the tree propagates by suckering and the twenty that surround you are the hydra heads thrown up when some earlier monster was decapitated. Chop it down? Your axe rebounds from the hard, springy wood. Saw it down? Then be sure to wear a stout glove to protect the back of your hand. Drag it off to the bonfire and burn it? You can try but in six months it will still be there mocking your efforts. Does its gay blossom herald the approach of spring? On the contrary it usually coincides with a spell of icy weather appropriately known as 'blackthorn winter'. As for its fruit, Eve's apple was not more tempting – nor more bitter. Finally, in late autumn the hedge cutter comes along our narrow lane and trimmings of blackthorn lie in the roadway. Vindictive to the last! You drive over it at your peril.

So I massacred it without mercy until victory was mine. Then I surveyed the battlefield. What remained? There were several hazels, a small oak tree and a small sycamore. On the other slope were two mature oaks. With pruning saw and secateurs I tidied them all up and gave them my blessing.

I was now at the top, lord of all my lands. If a few patches of uncleared scrub still remained, these could await my pleasure. But if my path had reached its destination, I had yet to establish a reason for coming here. So I levelled another area, a rather larger one this time, about ten feet across. If you think of it as roughly square, then on one side the ground rose to the hazel-topped hedgebank that formed the left-hand boundary of our land, and on another side it rose to the stone wall that formed our right-hand boundary. Behind this wall was a spinney of oaks. The third side faced back down the hill I had climbed. The fourth side justified all my efforts. Here the ground dropped away over the steeper of my two triangles to give a magnificent view down the narrow valley that led to the sea.

Such a place clearly demanded a seat.

Down in the house was a great oak beam. It was nine inches square and eight feet long. It had served, I suspect, a variety of purposes in the course of its life, but recent alterations to our fireplace had left it temporarily without a home. Well, here was as good a home as any I was likely to be able to offer it. It was immensely heavy. I roped it to a little trolley and set to work hauling it up the hillside.

I got it to the top and hoisted it on to a couple of oak uprights sunk into the ground. I put it along the side that faced my view. Here it served two purposes. It was a seat, and you could face either outwards or inwards as you pleased. It was also a rampart or parapet and gave a sense of protection to one of the exposed sides of my site.

Perhaps because it was almost the only level area on our land, and perhaps too because subconsciously we felt ourselves to be mountaineers or explorers and so needed to establish our conquest in the appropriate way, here we hoisted our flag and set up our camp. And here in the course of the next few summers we would come with sleeping-bags and torches to spend an occasional pleasant if slightly restless night. Eventually both the tent and the pleasure it gave came to an end; but it left us with a name. The place from then on was known as 'the camp site'.

Over to the right, beyond the seat, is the ridge where the two triangular faces meet; and at this point the steeper, rockier slope starts with a vertical drop of about four feet to a more or less level terrace. This, almost certainly, is where the stone was quarried for the wall which, as I have already said, forms our right-hand boundary. When we first saw it, the rock face was crumbling and the terrace overgrown with brambles and bracken, and the loose stones that littered the area gave it a rather derelict air.

It was when I was beginning to plan my second book that I set to work to clear it up. I intended to build here a wooden hut, and the writing of my book and the building of this hut seemed to have some sort of symbolic connection. But though the book was finished and the site was levelled and tidied, the hut was not even started. I had designed it; I had even bought some of the wood for it; but in the end I found I didn't want it. I wanted only another wooden seat, and this eventually I made. Of the hut all that survives is its name, for this second levelled area became known as the 'hut site'. Although its shape is different – it is much longer and thinner – it too has the feeling of being enclosed on three sides, open on the fourth. The view is different: across the second valley to the great hill on the other side. Here one can sit and watch the sun go down, and notice how, as autumn moves towards winter, it drops behind the hedge each day a little further to the left.

Such was the camp site and the hut site, and I dearly loved them both. I would visit them, favouring now the one, now the other, depending upon the weather or my mood, sitting there for perhaps half an hour, perhaps only a few minutes. Sometimes I might come with spade and sickle to work among my trees, sometimes with bread and cheese to eat my lunch, sometimes with a cushion to lie on the ground and sleep, sometimes with binoculars to see what I could see, sometimes with nothing, just to contemplate. But much as I loved these two places, I was never happy about their names.

'Camp site' kept alive the memory of our Boy Scout tent. And the word 'hut' suggested those wooden sheds offered by mail order firms and erected by handymen in their back gardens. So when I wanted to refer to the hut site in my book, *The Path Through the Trees*, I left it anonymous. And now that I was again writing a book – what I had intended to be a sort of natural history of Embridge – there seemed no reason why it should not remain anonymous.

You cannot write a book without being influenced by other books, and I knew that there was one in particular that would influence me: Richard Jefferies' *Wild Life in a Southern County*. I liked the way it had started: in a hollow on a hillside, an ancient excavation on the Marlborough Downs known as Liddington Castle. Though the scale was altogether different, this hollow seemed to have something in common with my two hollowed-out areas . . . and then as I pondered on this I saw in a flash how much more there was in common than I had supposed and how mistaken I had been about those two names.

All at once I saw that both 'camp' and 'hut', so far from

being wrong, were in fact peculiarly appropriate. For both had other, very much older meanings.

By 'camp' we can also mean the old Roman *castra* or fortification. 'Hut' can refer to the dwellings of the prehistoric inhabitants of Dartmoor. And 'site' is of course the word we use to describe what remains of such places. Though they were naturally only miniatures, one could almost believe that here at Embridge was once quartered a Roman legion guarding the valley road, and here, protected alike from the weather and from marauders, Iron Age man went about his business. Oddly enough, sitting here and looking out across the valley, I had had precisely that feeling of protection and security from attack that these people would have needed. Indeed on a number of occasions I had found myself imagining enemy troops moving across the hill opposite. Quite unconsciously, it seemed, I had been reconstructing the past. Why?

I dug out my copy of *Wild Life* to see if Jefferies could suggest an answer. Here is how it begins.

The most commanding down is crowned with the grassy mound and trenches of an ancient earthwork, from whence there is a noble view of hill and plain. The inner slope of the green fosse is inclined at an angle, pleasant to recline on, with the head just below the edge, in the summer sunshine.

Wasn't there something familiar about this? Didn't he begin another book in much the same way? Again I searched for my copy. It was *The Story of My Heart*. It begins with a description of the three-mile walk from his home at Coate; then comes the gradual climb up the short sweet turf of the downs, and finally his arrival at the entrenchment on the summit. He climbs down into it, walks around it slowly to recover breath, then stretches himself out on the grass. He is alone now and can meditate.

> I was utterly alone with the sun and the earth. Lying down on the grass I spoke in my soul to the earth, the air, and the distant sea far beyond sight. I thought of the earth's firmness – I felt it bear me up; through the grassy couch there came an influence as if I could feel the great earth speaking to me . . .

Thus from his hollow on the Marlborough Downs Jefferies could be on one occasion the naturalist, observing and recording, and on another occasion the philosopher-poet, sensing and dreaming. One does indeed need to be both, for the one complements and enhances the other. The single-minded naturalist who is scientist only – peering through his magnifying glass at one of life's lesser organisms, too preoccupied to notice the way the shadows fall on the hillside opposite – misses much. But so, too, does the single-minded poet, seeing only beautiful, beautiful trees and not knowing oak from ash, his eye skimming joyfully over the landscape, not knowing when to stop and peer more closely, where to search and find.

I had started out with every intention of being the scientist. But now Jefferies was deflecting me. In what direction I was still unsure. I knew only that I was feeling again the explorer's urge to be up and away on another expedition into the unknown. I had two possible bases from which I might start, reason on one side and emotion on the other. I would try reason first, and, since he had been so much help to me earlier, I would begin in the company of Karl Pearson.

3   *Reason*

Karl Pearson was a mathematician. Mathematics is pure logic, absolute truth, absolute certainty, no guesswork, no speculation. The mathematician makes his own world and in it he is god. Perhaps his world bears some likeness to the real world, but it is not obliged to do so. Within it he establishes his own rules, as Euclid established the axioms of his geometry. From this all else follows. Theorem after theorem can be proved with uncontradictable certainty.

Science too, argued Pearson, dealt in certainties. But the starting point of the scientist was the outside world. What do we know of the outside world? Nothing beyond what our various senses report to us and our brain records – 'sense impressions', as Pearson called them. The outside world is nothing but a mass of sense impressions stored away in the mind of man. It was the task of the scientist to collect and catalogue a particular range of these sense impressions – as it might be those connected with falling apples or twinkling stars – to isolate that feature they all had in common and to express it as concisely as he could in a simple description. Science *described*. It did not *explain*. And a 'scientific law' was 'a brief description in mental shorthand of as wide a range as possible of the sequences of our mental impressions'. It was a description of past observations which could then be used to predict future observations. If this sounds to the unscientific a little complicated, let me illustrate what I mean by the homely fable of the Man Who Went Shopping.

This man was a scientist. If his misfortunes leave us smiling in a superior way at his naivety, so much the better: it is good for our morale to find there are things that we know and scientists don't. But we must appreciate that on this occasion the law he is investigating is not one of nature's. It is one of man's. We know the answer. And so we, god-like, can watch him stumbling his way towards the truth.

He lived in the depths of the country and, since he lived alone and since even scientists must eat, he did all his own shopping. The village grocer being several miles away, these expeditions took up much valuable time. He did not have a car; the hills were too steep for a bicycle; and no bus service came his way. So he walked. And even though he would set out as soon as he had breakfasted, it was lunch time before he was home again – a whole morning away from his laboratory. He therefore planned his shopping list so as to keep to the minimum the number of these expeditions.

Such was his routine and all went well until one day, much to his surprise, he arrived at the shop to find it shut. Here was both a puzzle and a great annoyance. He would now have nothing for lunch and he would have to make the journey again the following day. Another morning wasted. Also it introduced an element of uncertainty into his life. For his law of shopping ('Shop open') had failed him.

He went again the next day, a little apprehensively, but all was well. And all was well on the next three occasions. But on his fourth visit he found the shop once again shut. His routine was now thoroughly upset. His journeys out were filled with anxiety, his journeys back were filled all too often with nothing but a sense of frustration.

Being a scientist he realized that a law that no longer

gave accurate predictions was worthless. A new one was needed to take its place and he must carry out a series of observations until one suggested itself. He was aware that, though his problem might be relatively easy, it might equally well be virtually insoluble. For instance, the shop might close whenever the shopkeeper needed to visit his local wholesaler to replenish stock and this might occur at intervals that followed no predictable pattern.

No longer now did he visit the shop as seldom as possible. He needed to go as often as his other work would allow, and so every two or three days saw him setting off over the hills to make another recording. The year advanced. Spring became summer. Summer became autumn. And then suddenly, blindingly, the answer came to him. So simple it was. So obvious, really, once you knew. Such a neat little law. $C_n = C_o + 7n$, where C is closing day and n is any integer.

Or, as we would put it, 'Closed on Sundays'.

Is that the end of the story? No, indeed. For we with our superior knowledge can see that his new law will remain valid only so long as he arrives at the shop before one o'clock. He has yet to discover 'Closed 1 to 2.15' and 'Early closing Wednesday'. And, more difficult still, he has to learn about 25 and 26 December, Good Friday, Easter Monday and the effect of leap years.

For him many years of research still lie ahead. For us it is enough to notice three things. First: how hard it is to recognize the pattern that lies behind even the simplest of phenomena, especially if our observations are not continuous. Secondly: the need to be constantly modifying our law as our observations increase in range and accuracy. Thirdly: the fact that our law merely describes. It does not explain. An explanation of *why* the village shop was shut every seventh day would range from Genesis to the Shops Act and no amount of observation would disclose it.

Having watched a scientist trying to make sense of the laws of man, let us now watch him at work on the laws of nature. Let us accompany him into the darkness and look up at the sky. If the night is cloudless, various tiny points of light will be visible and, in addition, there may be a larger patch of light more or less circular in shape.

You can call the large object the moon and the smaller ones stars, and you can say that the moon and the stars move across the sky every night. As night follows night this movement changes a little. The moon changes shape and rises each evening a little later. There is a simple pattern here, the phases of the moon, a cycle that repeats itself roughly every thirty days. Yet the repeats are not identical. Each month the moon behaves a little differently as the year moves through the seasons. In other words there is a daily cycle which is grafted on to a monthly cycle which is grafted on to an annual cycle. This is as far as my own observations take me and so for me is a good enough approximation to the truth. But if you study the movements of the moon a little more closely you will find that even the annual patterns do not repeat themselves exactly and in fact you have to wait nineteen years before you are really back at the beginning again. This nineteen-year period is known as the Metonic cycle.

For me it is enough to know that the moon rises about an hour later each night. Armed with this information I can predict that tomorrow, if the sky is clear, it will be coming up through the branches of the plane tree around seven o'clock – just right for a moonlit walk along to the beech avenue before supper. But if I wanted to know where the moon was going to be at seven o'clock on New Year's Day 1985, I would need a more accurate knowledge of the pattern. I would need to stand back a little and see how it varied not just from day to day, not just from month to month but from year to year.

All this is simple enough. More than two thousand years ago the Chaldeans – those wise men from the east whose interest in stars once led them to Bethlehem – were familiar with the Metonic cycle. What about the much more complicated weavings of the planets? What sort of pattern do they follow? Where will Venus be at seven o'clock on New Year's Day 1990?

Here the pattern only begins to come clear if we stand back not in time but in space. Stand back and visualize the earth not as something flat that extends to the horizon and then stops but as a giant sphere with the sun and the stars all travelling *round* it. That helps immensely. But it is even better if you stand further back and picture not the earth but the sun as the centre of the universe. Then the still fairly complicated movements of the planets really do become simple to describe. They move in ellipses round the sun as focus, and so does the earth. Kepler summed it all up – describing not only their paths but also their fluctuating speeds – in three brief laws. Seventy years later Newton reduced the three to one, a single sentence that tells us exactly what Venus has done in the past and what she will do in the future. $F = Gmn/d^2$.

$F = Gmn/d^2$. That's all there is to it. Armed with this piece of information and a few observations, it is possible to calculate all you want to know about the movements of the planets, the moon and the sun for the next thousand-odd years. Is this then the law that rules them? No. It is the law that rules the behaviour of 'particles' in the imaginary world that Newton invented. Here it rules supreme and nothing can contradict it. From this law it is fairly easy to show (by which I mean that I have a recollection that I was once able to show it) that a small particle, given a certain initial velocity, will rotate around a larger one in an elliptical orbit and that it will in fact obey the three laws that Kepler had established by collecting and analysing the observations of his fellow astronomers. In Newton's world 'F' is the gravitational pull with which one particle attracts another, the force of gravity. Does this force exist up in the sky? Does the sun control the flying planets, pulling them towards her like dogs on an invisible lead? It is not for us to attempt to answer that question. As Pearson puts it: 'The law of gravitation is not so much the discovery by Newton of a rule guiding the motion of the planets as his invention of a method of briefly describing the sequences of sense impressions which we term planetary motion.'

Scientists are a restless lot, never content with a law but forever testing its accuracy, peering through their telescopes into the vastness of space, peering through their microscopes into the minutiae of matter, improving their tools so that they can see a little more clearly, measure a little more exactly and so test their predictions with greater precision. If one night the moon were to rise a second or two later than they had calculated they would want to adjust their law so as to encompass this new observation. Indeed they might even welcome it if the moon were a little late: it would be a puzzle to challenge them.

So complacency was shattered and excitement was stimulated when, round about the turn of the century, some puzzling things were noticed that seemed to throw doubt on currently held ideas on the nature of space and matter. The old law was failing. A new law was needed. And in the end Newton's world, so beautifully simple, so mathematically satisfying, ranging in its practical applications from apples to stars, predicting the future with such amazing accuracy, was seen for what Pearson, writing in 1892, had said it was, no more than a man-made world and by no means necessarily the only world that man could make to match his sense impressions. Einstein's world, a four-dimensional space-time continuum twisting about in a total of ten dimensions, could do it just as well and on occasion rather better. Where Newton's world was ruled by 'force' and the neat little law, $F = Gmn/d^2$, Einstein's was ruled by 'curvature' and the equally neat little formula $G_{\mu\nu} = \lambda g_{\mu\nu}$. Force or curvature, which is it really?

It is all a little like the Welsh tapestry quilts we once used to sell in our bookshop. At first glance they seemed to have a pattern that consisted of an arrangement of squares, but when you stood back a little you saw instead a pattern of circles. Which was it really? If you had asked the weaver he could doubtless have written out the formula according to which he had set up his loom. But would that have left you any the wiser? Squares or circles: it is for you to say. Force or curvature? Again the choice is yours.

As I lay on my bunk with *The Grammar* back in 1941 I saw at once how right Pearson was. Be content to discover *what*. Don't try to guess *why*. Here was an attitude that combined both pride and humility: pride in the power of the human intellect; humility in admitting its limitations. I knew now how far reason could take me and I would go no further. Better than any set of ready-made answers, what Pearson had given me was the apparatus for testing such answers as might be offered to me. Did they depend upon evidence that no scientist would accept, did they speculate more deeply than science would allow? Then I would reject them. Were the arguments dressed up in scientific language? Then I was at once on my guard. I was not going to be deceived by the pseudo-science of the unscientific.

But Pearson went further than that, and though I followed him loyally at the time, I found, on re-reading his *Grammar* more recently, that I could no longer do so. For he goes on to claim for science that 'the whole range of phenomena, mental as well as physical – the entire universe – is its field', and that 'the scientific method is the sole gateway to the whole region of knowledge'. For 'minds trained to scientific methods are less likely to be led by mere appeal to the passions or by blind emotional excitement to sanction acts which in the end may lead to social disaster.'

I shall be arguing later on that a blind following of reason is just as likely to lead to social disaster as is a blind following of emotion. But for the moment I would like to look a little more closely at his statement that the scientific method is the sole gateway to the whole field of knowledge. Here I am going to agree with him, but (let me quickly add) not because I think there is anything peculiar or superior in the scientific method. Rather I am going to argue that it is nothing more than the normal way in which all human brains function. There is nothing that the scientist can teach mankind about his techniques that mankind has not already taught the scientist. From the time we get up to the time we go to bed we are all scientists.

What is the purpose of the brain? How do animals that possess one differ from plants that do not? In this way. The plant takes the world as it comes. It may well react to what comes, closing its petals when the sun goes behind a cloud. But it cannot anticipate events. It cannot say, 'The sun will shortly go behind a cloud. I would be wise to close my petals now in readiness.' To say this one needs a brain. A brain enables its owner to predict the future and so forestall events. The plant can only say, 'Here is water. I drink it.' The animal says, 'I can see water over there. If I go towards it, I shall be able to drink it.'

This immediately raises the question: how does an animal know that a certain pattern of light waves falling on the retina of the eye and transmitting along the optic nerve a message to the brain indicates the possibility of quenching the thirst? The answer is that the brain has a store of all past sense impressions that have been delivered to it and from these, like an efficient secretary, it is able to bring forward at once the file that contains those that have a similarity to the one now being reported. A certain pattern is observed; this pattern is isolated and the new impression is fitted into it to form a part of it. The rest of the pattern then indicates the likely course of future events. The simplest of patterns concerns events of two types, type A and type B. The store of past impressions – memory or experience, whichever we like to call it – reports that event A is always followed by event B. Hence when 'A' occurs, 'B' can be anticipated. Cause and effect, or, as Alice put it, 'If you cut your finger very deeply it usually bleeds.' And parents can watch their children at work painfully experimenting, learning the hard way, just as scientists do, until at last they have their law.

From a whole range of knife pictures the child isolates the characteristic of sharpness. At first perhaps the knife pictures need to have a strong family resemblance. In other words they must be pictures of the same knife. Later can be incorporated other knives that are more or less similar. Later still can be added a yet wider range of objects all of which possess certain features in common which enable them too to be placed in the folder labelled 'Knife'. And since one cay say of 'knife' that it is 'a brief description in mental shorthand of as wide a range as possible of the sequences of our sense impressions', one can fairly claim that it is as much a scientific law as $F = Gmn/d^2$.

Thus, by establishing law after law, we equip ourselves with the skills necessary for our survival. Much of the time what we do is done so quickly and so automatically that we are hardly aware of doing it. We do it, as we say, 'without thinking'. I walk down the road. Now and again my eyes glance ahead of me. From what they report I am able to predict that each time I put my foot on the ground it will land on something firm enough to support it and hold it steady. Left, right, left. The pattern is familiar. Left, right, left. It is so familiar that I can leave my feet to get on with it while my eyes and my thoughts turn to other, more interesting matters. This morning, however, my eyes reported something a little different. The surface of the road was shiny. From within the large folder labelled 'Road' my brain produced a smaller one labelled 'Shiny Road' and isolated a pattern that linked shininess with slipperiness. So now I could no longer assume that when I put my foot on the ground it would stay where I put it. It might well shoot from under me. I could no longer predict that I would remain upright. And at once walking became a slow and tedious business that called for all my attention.

From this we can see how immensely important to us are those things in our life that are stable and unchanging. So much of our world is in motion. How welcome are the bits that stand still. I find it quite hard enough to remember where, a moment ago, I put down my screwdriver. How very much harder life would be if screwdrivers behaved like Alice's croquet mallet and wandered off when left to themselves. When the sands shift how blessed is the solid rock. If we cannot have absolute changelessness let us at least hope to find in change an unchanging pattern, a cycle that repeats itself. I can predict that my house will be where I left it when I get home for lunch. I can predict this because houses do not move. I can also predict that a bus will draw up at the Dartmouth bus stop at a quarter past one able to carry me to Blackpool Sands. The bus moves but its movements follow a pattern that repeats itself every twenty-four hours. The exact pattern it follows, the law of motion that would completely describe its routine, I do not know or wish to know. I am concerned only with what lies between 1.15 and 1.45.

Thus the various laws that I extract from my surroundings and use to enable me to predict and anticipate are very limited in their range. I do not keep a whole bus timetable in my mind, only a single entry. And so it is with the scientists. What have they discovered about the world? Only what human beings want to find and are able to find, only those things that can be measured, that do not change or whose change follows some unchanging pattern. They can measure length and time and mass. They cannot, so far as I know, measure taste or smell or beauty, and one can hardly claim that their measurements of the length of sound waves tells us a great deal about the sound of music.

I have tried to show that what Pearson called the scientific method is nothing more than the method adopted by the human brain to keep its owner alive. Let me now go on to suggest that it is one of the methods adopted to keep its owner happy. For just as the body takes a delight in bodily activities so does the brain take a delight in brainy activities. And since the brain's main function is to sort and catalogue (albeit often unconsciously), sorting and cataloguing in one form or another is an activity that gives us much innocent pleasure.

Over my thirty years as a bookseller I have spent long and happy hours sorting and cataloguing books. Here is a pile of them, several thousand, a mixed lot, all the books in my shop thrown together and stirred up. Now put them in order. Make sense of them so that you can predict where you will find the one you want. It would be interesting to see how each person tackled this particular task. There is no one right way, not even one best way. It depends for a start on the purpose for which the books are needed. It might well be that we need them for building a barricade behind which to shelter. Books make admirable bricks. In that case we would sort them according to size, all books of the same size in the same pile. But then how would we arrange our piles? Books have three dimensions. Would we group together those piles that possessed a common width or a common height? It would depend of course on the particular method of bonding that we favoured.

I like to think that the books I sell are mostly going to be used not for building but for reading and so I am concerned not only with size but also with content. This adds a complication. And a further complication is that I am arranging them partly for my benefit, so that I can make my predictions, and partly for the benefit of my customers, so that they can make theirs. An arrangement that suits me doesn't always suit them. Books can be arranged by author, by title, by subject, by series, by publisher, by age and by size; and perhaps the surprising thing is that, from time to time, from place to place and for one reason or another, I use *all* these methods.

Thus the scientist in the bookshop; and if he has a lesson to teach us it is, I think, to emphasize once again that the scientist behind the telescope is not so much discovering the laws of nature as selecting for observation those phenomena that interest him. He likes to think that he has removed individual human bias from his observations and deductions, but he knows he can never remove the bias of being human. A scientifically-minded insect would have reached quite different conclusions about the world.

Now let us look at the scientist at Embridge. Here he might call himself a naturalist.

Round about the age of thirteen I developed a passion for birds; and at Cotchford where my family lived and at Stowe where I went to school that passion had all the opportunity it needed. Fields, woods, hedges, streams and lakes were all within an afternoon's ramble. No matter that I knew nothing of the birds that haunt the rocky coasts and river estuaries. I had enough here to keep me happy; and away I would go on my own with my binoculars over my shoulder.

To the beginner all small brown birds are sparrows and

'chirrup chirrup' is what they say; but gradually, just as the astronomer learns to tell a planet from a star and then one planet from another, so I learned to distinguish finches from warblers, and the marsh tit from the coal-tit. And instead of filing away in my mind a folder labelled 'Birds' I had separate folders for each species. All this was done exactly as the scientist does it, exactly as we all do it. My 'coal-tit' was no more a particular coal-tit than were Newton's 'particles' particular bits of matter or the diction-ary's 'knife' a particular knife.

Gradually my folders grew more numerous. Was it indeed a Dartford warbler that I saw one afternoon in Ashdown Forest? I liked to think it was. At Stowe I added redstart, little owl, reed bunting and reed warbler to my list. But once I had seen and identified a redstart I didn't particularly need to see another. I would rather find something new. And since one cannot hope to find a new species of bird on every expedition, what I searched for were nests. Nests were sufficiently hard to find – two or three being all I could hope for in the course of an outing – that even another blackbird's was a discovery worth making.

So each year I went hunting. The nesting season began at Cotchford at the beginning of the Easter holidays, began with the mistle thrush and those first nests that wrens make before they have decided which one to line with feathers. I was at Cotchford until early May and by that time my collection might include a nuthatch, a long-tailed tit and a chaffinch. Then on to Stowe where the season would last until around half term. At Stowe the nest I found most often was the whitethroat's, but I have memories of reed warbler, redstart, chiff-chaff, willow warbler and spotted flycatcher. It was nests I collected, not eggs; and I collected them mentally, not physically in any way, not even to record them in a diary, just to remember them. This is the best way. The egg collections of our youth seldom survive to enrich our middle age. Whereas my nest memories, neatly filed and readily accessible, are still in excellent condition.

Today I no longer consider myself an ornithologist. Where I now live I cannot so easily wander through fields and woods and beside streams. Also I am older and might feel uneasy if someone came upon me squatting on the ground peering into a thicket. Today I watch birds in a more casual way. If one appears at Embridge that I do not at once recognize I like to try and identify it. Once when my wife and I were driving to work a bird flew up from just ahead of us, followed the lane for a short distance, then rose and dropped over the hedge and out of sight. What was it? I noticed a brownish orange back and a black-and-white rump that made a sort of chequerboard pattern. A jay – yet not a jay because the pattern was wrong. My wife noticed a long beak. A woodpecker – yet not a woodpecker because the colouring was wrong. Answer: a hoopoe. Rare visitor though he is, I had no doubt whatever. That was something to remember. But I take my hoopoes as they come. I don't go looking for them. I keep an ear open for the first chiff-chaff, the first willow warbler and the first blackcap, happy to welcome them back to Embridge. I like to watch buzzards wheeling in the sky overhead and to be out of doors on a winter's night when the owls are hooting to each other. But it is years since I found a nest.

Today I am more interested in wild flowers and insects. But I still do not pretend to be very expert. I do not hunt particularly diligently nor do I examine my finds under a microscope. It is enough if I can name them, if I can summarize my 'wide range of sense impressions' by the single word 'pennywort'. It is not only satisfying, it is also good manners to know one's neighbours by name. I often wish I could name my fellow humans with equal certainty.

Let us watch the botanist at his studies. It is early March. I climb the path that leads to the camp site and my eyes report a small spot of pale yellow under the hazels. It might be the top of a cider bottle. It might be the planet Venus. It might be a flower. I'll settle for a flower: it is the most likely. In that case it might be a potentilla or it might be a pansy or it might be a primrose. I'll settle for primrose: it is the most likely. Actually I must confess that I knew it was a primrose all along: primroses grow on this particular slope in their hundreds, and my brain had produced the 'primrose' file without a moment's hesitation. It hadn't even bothered to mention any of the other possibilities.

My primrose file is a fat one, beginning well back in my childhood and containing annual additions, right up to last summer. Thus I am able to predict what I shall find if I approach a little closer – the shape of the leaves, the way they grow, the shape of the flower head and the way the young buds cluster together in the centre of the plant. I couldn't give a scientific description of it all, but I can visualize in advance the softness of the leaf and the spider's web pattern of its wrinkles, the downy stem of the flower and the way the yellow buds seem to squeeze through the – what's the word? – calix, like – Well, it's a little like the way that, after you have put a shelled almond into hot water, you can squeeze its white kernel through its loose brown skin. Or is it the other way round, and does the almond remind me of the primrose? Also it's like something else that I can't quite recall. Come on, brain! More files! More pattern books!

I go up to the primrose and look down at it. Yes, I was right. It matches. And as I look so I see not just its single yellow face but a million primroses, all those I have ever seen in my life. Some of them have labels round their necks giving me information about where and when I met them and any special circumstance connected with the occasion.

Add all this together – to get what Pearson called a 'construct' – and you have rather more than the 'low hairy perennial with tapering leaves' which (with a bit more in the same style) is the 'brief description in mental shorthand' that the botanist gives me.

It is very hard to be the single-minded naturalist, seeing only *primula vulgaris* when you are on a hillside in spring. It is hard to suppress the stirrings of emotion. But before I finish with reason I must briefly sum up my discoveries.

I have shown that Rational Man has much in common with the scientist. Both use past experiences to plan or predict future events. The scientist does this deliberately, painstakingly, recording on paper the results of his experiments. Rational Man is more inclined to rely on memory and jumps rather quickly to conclusions. 'Once bitten, twice shy' is good enough for him. The only essential difference between the two is that the scientist's truths are always general truths – those from which the individuality of the observer has been eliminated, those to which all must therefore agree – while rational truths include personal truths. Thus, 'drinking prussic acid always makes one ill' is a general truth confirmed by all who have carried out the experiment, whereas 'eating oysters always makes me ill' is a personal truth.

Both Rational Man and the scientist when they are trying to make sense of a range of experiences construct a model. It is this model, not the reality, that they then study. Such models can be mental, verbal or pictorial, occasionally even three dimensional. The commonest is a mental picture (based on experience) of what something looks like, so that when we see it again we recognize it. But the models we make do not need to resemble the reality we are contemplating. They include such things as maps, timetables, diagrams, descriptions, instructions. Even the words we use are models. The word 'moon' is not the actual moon, nor does it in the least resemble it, either when written or when spoken. You cannot say of a model that it is 'true' or 'false', only that it does or does not serve its purpose. This purpose can be very limited. It can be limited to the person making it – as is a mental picture of something – or to that person and the person he is talking to – as are verbal instructions – or to that person and others who understand his language – as are printed instructions. Obviously if we wish to convey an idea to another person the model we make must be one that he will interpret in the same way as we do.

In this chapter I have been trying to understand the process of reasoning. To do this I have made a mental model of the brain which I can put into words by saying that it is a little like an office filing system. It is a model that I have found helpful, and naturally I hope that others too will find it helpful. In my next chapter I will be enlarging on it. But it will remain a model with a limited purpose: to understand the motives that direct men's actions. It will be of no use at all to a surgeon wishing to carry out a lobotomy, who will need for his purpose an altogether· different model.

And now, having explored reason as far as I can, I must cross over to the other side and see what I can discover about emotion.

4 *Emotion*

When I was a child I never lost my temper. This, perhaps the most distressing of all childhood emotions, was one that I was mercifully spared. But I suffered from most of the others. I burst into tears on too many occasions for too little reason. I could be jealous and resentful and unbearably shy. And I knew what it was to be afraid. I was afraid of the dark. I was afraid of witches. At school I was afraid of boys who liked hitting other boys on the nose. I was very far from brave.

So, like most of us at that age, I looked upon my emotions as inner, painful and rather unmanly things that I must do my best to conceal.

I was little more than a schoolboy when war came. I no longer cried but I could still feel afraid. Would I feel afraid? In peace time this is not a question that need bother a young man. If he feels the urge to test his courage he can look for a mountain and climb it, look for an ocean and sail it, or buy a fast car and drive it to the terror of other road users. But he has no need to do such things. At school I had happily left it to others to be heroic on the rugger field. If the war had not come I have no doubt that I would have been just as happy to leave mountains, oceans and fast cars to others. No one would have pointed a finger at me and cried, 'Coward!'

But the war left me no option. Here was a challenge, a

test of my physical courage that I must not avoid; for I knew that if I did I could never forgive myself.

In 1941 my battles still lay ahead of me: battles with Germans, maybe; battles almost certainly with fear. It was the latter that I had to win, and I was pleased with myself that, at least in prospect, I was not afraid. I was pleased that, on the whole, I seemed able, for the first time in my life, to keep my emotions under control.

Yes, emotions had to be controlled. It was childish to give way to anger. It was girlish to give way to tears. And soldiers did not give way to fear. I was grown up now, no longer childish, no longer girlish. I was a soldier and in command of myself. And so when in the summer of that year I came upon Pearson arguing that reason should be our sole guide in every field of human experience and that we should not be 'led by mere appeal to the passions or by blind emotional excitement', I agreed with him, not only as a fellow mathematician but also as a man.

For it is not only the rationalist who likes to think himself a rational human being. We all do – especially men. We are (rightly) proud of our ability to reason, to think logically. We are (excusably) a little ashamed if inadvertently we display our emotions rather too publicly. 'Mere' emotion. 'Unrestrained' emotion. Those childhood memories still haunt us. If we hold a belief, it is, we firmly claim, a rational belief. No, no. It is absurd to suggest that it might be a 'mere' emotional belief; and so we do our best to scratch together rational arguments in support of it.

It was when, in 1964, I came upon Macmurray's *Reason and Emotion* that I began to see how our emotions were being underrated. We had two guides, not one, two voices whispering in our ear and prompting our actions. Nor was reason necessarily the senior partner. There were of course many occasions when the voice of reason was to be preferred. But there were other occasions when reason was unable to advise us and we must listen instead to the voice of emotion. Reason depended upon experience – which was why in our childhood, lacking experience of the world, we had to rely so much on emotion. Experiences, to be of any value to us, had to possess something in common. It was this common factor that enabled us to make our predictions. Reason therefore worked best in the mechanical world where things ran true to expectation. But much of the world was not mechanical. The moon's behaviour was mechanical; man's behaviour was not. Man's behaviour was often emotional, unpredictable, following no known laws. But here, where reason gives us least assistance, emotion comes to our rescue. It is emotion that determines our relations with our fellow men, and our closest personal relationships are almost wholly emotional. Emotion guides us elsewhere too. The astronomer may tell us something about the moon, but so too does the poet. The astronomer's moon is everybody's moon; the poet's is very much his own and not everyone can share it with him.

I was up at the camp site contemplating the primroses that were then just coming into flower. I could look at them with the eye of reason, the botanist's eye, or I could look at them with the eye of emotion, the artist's eye. I thought I understood how the brain rationalized on what the eye saw. I had made a model of the brain based on an office filing system. But as yet I had not tried to understand the workings of emotion. I had kept the two quite separate, so as not to confuse them. I had – as most people do – located reason in the head and emotion in the heart, an elementary model that served its very limited purpose. Perhaps the time had come to attempt something more complicated. Perhaps the primroses might suggest something.

Devon is famous for the profusion of its primroses. They

grow not just in woods and along hedgebanks as in other counties. They grow also in open fields and can turn a grassy hillside as yellow as daisies can turn it white. Not surprisingly, during our first years in Devon when spring came round and the hills became yellow, I felt the familiar thrill that I had first experienced when I was a child at Cotchford. I had experienced it very strongly then. I was experiencing it almost as strongly now. And so it continued to be, year after year, until one year, well into the month of May, I suddenly realized that the primrose season was almost over – and I had scarcely noticed it.

Shortly after that I began to write *The Enchanted Places* and this meant making a deliberate effort to unearth childhood memories in order to describe them; and it was then that I found myself thinking of Wordsworth's 'Immortality' ode. How very true! The vision that one saw as a child with such piercing clarity does indeed fade as one grows older.

At the time I merely recorded in my book that this was so. It was not until quite recently that I asked myself where this vision came from and why it faded. I searched around for a moment or two, then came up with an answer.

The first thing I realized was something I mentioned towards the end of the last chapter: there is nothing in a blob of yellow to tell the eye anything. The eye is simply the postman that carries the message to the brain. Nor is there anything in the message itself for the brain to get excited about. The excitement comes when the folders are produced and the previous correspondence is studied. It is like the letter that merely says 'I agree': it is meaningless until one refers back to discover what is agreed. Thus the primrose I contemplate at any time is not only that particular flower but all the others I have ever seen; and I am thus reminded also of the various occasions on which

I saw them. Since primroses meant a lot to me as a child, I am reminded of my childhood. Thus the thrill I feel today – such as it is – is in part the stirrings of memory, the echo of an older thrill. But what about the thrill I felt as a child? What memories were there then? The six-year-old could perhaps look back a year or two. What about the four-year-old? At some point in time came the first primrose. Then what? The files were empty. No memory could be evoked. It was simply a pattern of colour to the eye, a soft feel between finger and thumb and a very slight sensation to the nose.

It is true that in retrospect those early primroses seem set in idyllic surroundings. But this has nothing to do with it. For if we can find nothing intrinsically thrilling in our first primrose how can there be anything intrinsically thrilling in the circumstances of that first meeting? If the primrose could stir no emotion, then neither could the wood where it grew.

So at what point *did* emotion enter the experience? As it is undoubtedly strong in childhood and appears to diminish as we grow older, I could only conclude that it was there from the start, that the primrose file was *not* empty at my birth. Something was already in it, something which, as the years went by and more and more correspondence was added, became increasingly hard to unearth. Memory is like a chain. We reach back into the past by a succession of links. I cannot necessarily remember a thing, but I remember remembering it. I am in contact with the intervening memory. Thus it is I have kept alive little pictures of my childhood, by repeatedly recalling them. I can get back so far but no further. It is like those ancient manuscripts that come down to us through copies of copies. I have an early copy, but the original, the document that was at the bottom of the file, is lost.

I had never bothered to think about such things before,

and now that I did so the explanation, as I have said, came quite suddenly. It was this.

The brain at birth is not, as I had supposed, an empty filing cabinet. It already contains a store of memories acquired and accumulated by preceding generations. In animals this is known as instinct. In humans, although certain animal instincts survive more or less unchanged, others have been refined and these have become our emotions. The emotion I felt on seeing my first primrose came from the inherited memory of primroses seen by my ancestors.

It was at this point that I abandoned my projected natural history of Embridge.

Let me first consider instinct.

A dog growls and the child, encountering a dog for the first time in its life, instinctively recoils. Another dog growls and a different child, remembering the time a growling dog once bit it, recoils for good reason. In both cases the brain receives messages from eyes and ears and in consequence sends out instructions to the body. The second set of instructions is clearly the result of memory; and so it was easy to persuade myself that the first set, apparently so similar, was the result of some sort of 'memory' too. In this case it could only be a 'memory' that was present at birth. I therefore called it 'inherited memory'.

Instinct, I argued, is inherited memory. Without it the brain would be a filing system with no files. The senses would send in their messages and the messages would have no meaning. All knowledge would have to come gradually by trial and error, and any error would be instantly fatal. No species could survive its earliest days without the closest attention from its parents, attention a great deal closer than is given by the mother fish to its fry or by the butterfly to its caterpillar children. Hence the immediate need for an instinct that will advise on food, on shelter and on avoiding enemies.

How is this instinct acquired? It is obviously acquired by previous generations and handed on to their offspring. But this doesn't quite answer the question. For it could still be acquired in two different ways. It could be the result of 'natural selection' the 'survival of the fittest'. This is the way (so I was taught) in which protective colouring is acquired. Those without it are eaten. Those with it stand a better chance of bringing up a family. Protective instinct could be acquired in the same way. Those who froze best lived longest. Thus the instinct to freeze could grow over the centuries in a series of jerks, each generation being a little better than the preceding one. Alternatively – and this is the theory I prefer – it could grow more gradually, day by day, hour by hour, minute by minute, as a steady stream of experience flows into the brain, is collected and is then – in some form – handed on.

To say this is not to suggest that I am protected against potentially fierce dogs by the memory of the dog that bit my father when he was a boy – any more than I would suggest that I could inherit from him the scar on his finger caused by that bite. But it is to suggest that there might be, at the very beginning of my 'Dog' file, some sort of précis of inherited experience that says, 'Beware of dogs that growl.'

Once I had persuaded myself of this I could see that instincts need not necessarily have any survival value at all. Consider kittens, for example.

Among our collection of cats we like to have at least one productive female and the consequence of this is a couple of litters every year. As this has been going on for over twenty years I can write about kittens with some authority.

One thing I have noticed is this. As soon as a kitten can open its eyes it will stare at me. As soon as it can crawl it

73

will drag itself towards me. As soon as it can run it will run to me and as soon as it can climb it will haul itself up my trouser leg. Why? You might have thought that a vast moving object would be something to hide from, not run towards. Yet instinct tells the infant kitten that this is not so; and this is an instinct that has nothing to do with survival. Later on in its life cat may come to depend on man, but the new-born kitten depends solely on its mother. However, if man is no protector, he is, almost immediately, tremendous entertainment value and the trousered leg soon becomes a wonderful adventure playground. For generation after generation – ever since cats first became domesticated –kitten and man have given each other endless pleasure. Is it fanciful to believe that memory of this lies at the back of every kitten's brain and is stirred the very moment man's dim shadow first looms into view? Fanciful or not, I was prepared to believe it.

The next thing I had to consider was the connection between instinct and emotion. There were obviously certain points where they touched. The instinct for self-preservation becomes the emotion of fear. The baby's instinctive cry for help becomes the crying of the child when it is upset. The miniature explosion that occurs when a kitten encounters an inquisitive dog becomes the explosion of temper we meet in children. Equally obviously both instinct and emotion, though they could be modified by experience, seemed to originate in some source that was outside experience. A seed of some sort was there at birth. The parallel seemed close enough and I now felt able to adapt my model of the human brain to describe the workings of both reason and emotion.

All human actions apart from reflex actions (I argued) originated in the brain and were of two kinds – and only two kinds – rational and emotional. Under 'emotional' I included 'instinctive' since there was no essential difference between the two. The brain records all experience, that is to say all the sense impressions it receives, and it files these away in what I pictured as a series of folders. Whenever a new message is received the brain instantly brings forward the appropriate folder and examines its contents to see what conclusions, if any, can be deduced and what actions, if any, are called for. At the bottom of each folder is an item that is different from all the others that lie on top of it. It is a précis, inherited at birth, of the two similar folders possessed by its parents. This précis will therefore have been conditioned by experiences going right back into our ancestral past.

Acquired memories can be examined one by one in the detached way of a scientist examining the results of his experiments. Inherited memory cannot be examined in this way. Instead it has a potency all its own. We *feel*. If the conclusions that can be drawn from an examination of acquired memories agree with the conclusion urged by inherited memory, all is well. But if the conclusions differ, then we have to decide between following 'our head' or 'our heart'.

That was my model. The next step was to see what could be deduced from it.

Because it is the custom for a woman on marriage to assume her husband's surname – because of this bias in favour of the male – we tend to think of our family tree as consisting of a single root linking a succession of fathers. Although it is usual for the family name, titles and estates to be passed along this male line only, family features and characteristics come equally from father and mother; and if we trace *these* backwards we find the number of our ancestors doubling at every generation. Thus, if there had been no intermarriage at all, we could claim a thousand million ancestors alive at the time of the Norman Conquest. Obviously this is an impossibility: the population of Europe at the time would not have allowed it. Obviously a lot of intermarriage between more or less distant cousins must have occurred. But at least this gives us an indication of the very widespread nature of our origins. We are like a tree whose roots, buried underground, divide and subdivide again and again as they spread outwards. And of course our neighbours are the same. Their roots too spread out and out and interlace with ours. We are like trees in a wood, our trunks quite separate one from another but beneath the soil an inextricably tangled network of fibres. The further away we get from the trunk, the finer and more numerous the fibres become and the more they intermesh. If one individual can claim up to a thousand million ancestors alive in 1066, then one Norman soldier can likewise claim a thousand million descendants alive today. And nine hundred years is the merest flicker of an eyelid in the history of mankind.

From this we can see how vast and how widespread is the source of our emotions. They come to us from as far south as the Mediterranean and from as far north as Scandinavia. The Phoenicians, the Romans and the Norsemen did not leave only their bones here, they left us their memories, and among them, no doubt memories of snow and ice, of mountains, of the sea, and of the desert sands.

The next thing to appreciate is simply that we are the survivors. Millions upon millions perished – died at birth, died soon after, failed to reach maturity, failed to mate and have children. But every single one of our millions upon millions of ancestors *all* succeeded, *all* lived to bring into the world at least one tough and healthy child. What a triumphant heritage is ours! What an amazing success story is our life! Did we fight battles? Then we won. Others may have been slain. Not us. Did pestilence or famine strike down our community? We survived it. Did we hazard our lives in some great enterprise? The risk paid off. Others may have been wrecked. We came safely ashore. Memories of childhood are ours, memories of youth, memories of gathering strength and growing towards maturity, memories of love. And there we stop. For at the moment of our conception the flow ceases. We know nothing of what follows, the gradual decline that leads in the end to death. We may see it in others. We do not know it in ourselves.

Is it then surprising that we love the world? The world was good to us. Through the woods and the fields, across the hills and the valleys, over the mountains and the moors and the sea we made our way in triumph. It is only in the last two hundred years that man has enclosed himself in towns. Is it likely that the preceding thousands will have been quite forgotten?

> There was a time when meadow, grove and stream,
> The earth and every common sight,
> To me did seem
> Apparelled in celestial light,
> The glory and the freshness of a dream.

This is our inheritance, the treasure of a hundred thousand years, collected by our ancestors and handed on to us at birth. What we do with it afterwards is another matter.

First memories are always the clearest. First day at school, first day of married life, first day in a new job, first view of Dartmouth. Later memories usually make less impression. They come flooding in and piling up, one on top of the other, so that the Dartmouth I glance at today is the Dartmouth I glanced at yesterday and the day before and the day before . . . Only if I make a conscious effort, or if the sun is just right, does it become the Dartmouth I first saw on that May morning thirty years ago. Later memories can obscure; but they can also keep alive. It depends how we use them.

When I was writing *The Enchanted Places* I remembered how much as a child I had loved daisies. Yet I had scarcely given them a glance since. Or rather I had glanced at them too often and with too little thought. Fortunately I had also glanced at them from too great a height – from a distance of five feet or more. A child is nearer to the ground and peers more closely. So I picked a daisy and looked at it as I had not looked at a daisy for over fifty years; and in the deep crimson tips to its petals I saw at once the daisies of my childhood. It was a sudden, dazzling revelation, a moment of vision and as near as I could ever deliberately get to that first daisy I had inherited at birth.

Thus by making this conscious effort did I re-establish a link with a childhood memory and thence to an emotion so deeply buried that I had forgotten its presence. It was as if I had opened up a long overgrown path. Today, no longer snared and distracted by the tangle of intervening memories, I can travel that way with greater ease. It still needs an effort but the effort is so much less. I know where the path lies and I know how to find its entrance.

'I was utterly alone with the sun and the earth. Lying down on the grass I spoke in my soul to the earth, the air, and the distant sea far beyond sight . . .'

In this way at Liddington Castle did Richard Jefferies find the entrance to his path, stretching himself out physically on the ground so that every part of him could feel the ground beneath bearing him up; stretching himself out spiritually until in imagination he touched the far horizon and could feel the great earth speaking to him.

I won't for one moment pretend that this is what I do at my camp site. I think I might feel a little embarrassed with myself if I did. But I know exactly how Jefferies felt; and I think I am now a little nearer to understanding why I feel that way too. Today we may look elsewhere for our shelter from the elements, for protection from marauders, for a place where we can worship our gods. But we have long memories. We have not forgotten!

5 Beauty

Not long ago I was reading Lord Hailsham's autobiography, *The Door Wherein I Went*, a book which, according to one of its reviewers, achieved 'classic excellence in the discussion and defence of Christianity'. In it, at one point, the author described his feelings at the sight of a beautiful landscape – the Alps, a bluebell wood, a field of daffodils. Such feelings, he said, had no survival value in the Darwinian sense and could not therefore be explained as having anything to do with man's evolution from the animal kingdom.

He went on to argue that for him they pointed to the existence of a divine creator. But he went on without me. Like man and dog out for a walk, we had put up a rabbit; and while he strode ahead oblivious, I stayed behind to investigate. Beauty. Evolution. Survival value. Here was a scent worth following; and in this chapter I shall follow it.

First I must say something about the world and its origins.

Little more than a hundred years ago there were two theories current in the west. The older theory pictured the world as relatively young and as having developed in a succession of disconnected jerks. The newer theory pictured it as a great deal older and as having developed continuously.

From the second theory it follows that if we identify certain characteristics possessed today by man, but not by the whirling mass of fiery vapour which is all there was at the beginning, these will have emerged gradually and not necessarily all at the same time. If, therefore, I try to trace man's social and mental development, it is quite possible that some of it will have already taken place before a creature visibly man-like appeared on the scene. Since it will be more convenient if I use the word 'man' throughout, it will be better if I give my model man a model world more like that in the older theory than in the newer. I will therefore be picturing human life as starting, if not quite with Adam and Eve in the Garden of Eden, at least with something very like it – a small tribe inhabiting a green valley in an unidentified country. This is the picture I would like the reader to keep at the back of his or her mind in the chapters that follow.

We have five senses. Although to some extent these senses collaborate in the work they do, each has its particular function in which it specializes. Thus our sense of touch is mainly concerned with the immediate protection of our body. Our senses of smell and taste help us to choose the right food. Our sense of sight informs us about the physical world in which we live. And our sense of hearing links us to our fellow men.

In this chapter I want to consider man in relation to his surroundings; and since our information about this comes to us mainly through our eyes the beauty I shall be investigating is visual beauty. Music may also be beautiful, but music must wait for a later chapter.

Memory is like money. We need money to provide us with the food and shelter necessary for our survival. When we are old enough we will no doubt be able to earn our own. But to begin with we must rely on what our parents provide, the money they have earned. We start, in other words, with inherited money. We may inherit a fortune. We may inherit the family business. We may inherit no more than enough to keep us in food and clothes until we leave school to earn our own living. Of what we inherit and of what we earn in the course of our life, some we spend and some we save to hand on to our own children when they arrive. Thus the penny I hold in my hand was perhaps earned by me or perhaps earned by my father or perhaps earned by some distant ancestor; and I may decide to spend it or I may give it to my daughter. So it is with memory. We start life with the memories we have inherited. To these we add new memories of our own. Some we retain. Some we forget. The balance, part inherited, part acquired, is handed on to our children. And just as there may be a distinction between the wealth we inherit and the wealth we earn, so there is a distinction between inherited and acquired memory. Acquired memory forms the basis of our reasoning, inherited memory of our emotions. Equally, whatever the distinctions, there remain the similarities. For what is inherited had first to be acquired. The emotions of today were the rationalizations of yesterday. And so, whether we are trying to understand reason or emotion, our starting point will be the brain and how it functions.

As I have already said, man's first need is to establish the fixed points in his world: the things that do not change and the things which, if they do change, change in a regular, predictable way. And this is true whether you are thinking of prehistoric man living in his cave and going hunting with his spear or modern man setting out from his semi-detached with brief case and rolled umbrella to catch the 7.45; whether you are thinking of the scientist in his laboratory or the child in his play-pen. We carry out our experiments, we store away our memories, we build up our files, we establish our certainties and we are thus able to make our predictions. And an early discovery we make is that the world we live in is not an exact one.

It is seldom that we can say more than 'It is extremely likely that . . .' or 'This is more or less how it will be.' Only when we look up into the sky do we find exactness. The planets move in exact ellipses. But when we lower our eyes and look at the world beneath our feet the ellipses we see are only approximate. I can throw a stone. In an ideal world the path it would follow would be a parabola. In our world air resistance causes it to fall short. I can drop my stone into a pond. In an ideal world the ripples would form circles. In our world they will be distorted both by the air and by the pond's shape. So we divide and sub-divide and classify and label, aiming at certainties but never achieving anything better than near-certainties. We look at trees and we notice that their leaves are different shapes. So we divide them into oaks and ashes and beeches and elms. We look at oak leaves. The differences now are less but they are still apparent. So we divide them into pedunculate oaks and sessile oaks – and *still* there are differences. No two oak leaves, even from the same tree, are ever absolutely identical.

So we learn to live with our approximations. Indeed we welcome them. We are after all a product of our world and its most successful product. We ourselves are a mass of approximations. It would be odd if we hadn't learned to profit from uncertainty.

If certainties were all he wanted, man would have got no further than the rest of creation. He would have stayed in the valley where he was born and felt no urge to climb the hill and explore the unknown valley on the other side. We need the security of our certainties but we need too the stimulus and the challenge provided by uncertainty. If we climb the hill it is not just in search of food; it is in search of adventure. Adventure calls and – as it turns out – how right we were to take the risk. For the valley on the other side was indeed greener. I don't mean that every valley is always greener than the last: just that ours was. Other adventurers may well have been less lucky and found only death waiting for them. But not us. Not our parents or our grandparents. We have always been lucky. If we hadn't, we wouldn't be here.

So, while the scientist inside us is recording his certainties, another part of us is welcoming the uncertainties. The scientist ties on his labels: Sun, Moon, Earth, Water, Oak, Ash . . . thousands upon thousands of labels, thousands upon thousands of groups and sub-groups, each with its set of ideal – but never exactly achieved – specifications. It is like a great army drawn up into regiments and battalions and companies and platoons. Or rather it is like two opposing armies, for some of the troops are friendly to us and some are hostile. And so when the scientist has finished his labelling we separate the friendly from the hostile, the beneficial from the harmful, and we add two more labels, two banners, one for each army. On one, for brevity, we will write the word 'Good' and on the other 'Bad'. And since we are human beings and the human race has been outstandingly successful in this world, it is not surprising that the good outnumber the bad. With the unhappy dinosaurs it was, in the end, the other way round.

We are grateful to the scientist for his work but there is just one thing he has left out. He was concerned only with the ideal. His labels define things as they ought to be. But the world is not ideal and so we need two further labels. The first says 'Small inexactnesses' and this we put with the good, and the second says 'Large inexactnesses' and this we put with the bad. Now all is complete. The centuries roll on their way. Sense impressions flood into the human brain are stored and are then handed on from parent to child. Yesterday's rationalizations become today's emotions. Good and bad are transformed into beautiful and ugly.

That, I believe, is how it came about: that is the origin of visual beauty.

There is a parallel with other senses. We need food and so we need to know what is good to eat and what is not. If the fruit we are contemplating is poisonous, it is helpful if we can discover this *before* we swallow it. And so we test it with our tongue. If it tastes pleasant we assume that it is good for us. If it tastes nasty we reject it. The advice given is not infallible but it serves us well enough. The nice taste of an apple is not something that resides solely within the apple; for not all creatures like apples. Its taste is rather the expression of a relationship between eater and eaten, a relationship that has developed over many generations, the accumulated experience of our ancestors that apples are good.

So whether we are gazing on a beautiful sight or savouring a delicious taste, we are profiting from the wisdom we inherit at birth – our guide to good and bad.

Armed with these thoughts, let us look at that familiar source of visual beauty, the human face.

As we contemplate the world around us, using for this purpose our eyes, we notice our fellow humans. We see them at a distance; they are part of the landscape; we are not necessarily going to enter into an intimate relationship with them all, but we need to know something about them. At this stage our eyes will give us the information we want and the face is where we will most readily find it.

A glance at the face serves two purposes. First, it helps us to distinguish one human from another, and secondly it tells us something about its owner. In this latter respect it is a little like the dust jacket of a book. It is a quick guide to what lies within. We look at the eyes: this man is kind. We look at the mouth: this man is cruel. One man smiles:

we go towards him. Another scowls: we run away. From all the varieties of human face and its association with human character we can in theory arrive at a definition of the 'standard handsome male' and the 'standard beautiful female'. These two standards will of course differ from country to country. Let us look a little more closely at the female. Yes, she is indeed beautiful. She has all the features that we have learned to associate with someone who is kind and loving and sweet-tempered and who is likely to make a loyal wife and a good mother. But to be honest we are not tremendously attracted to her. Her beauty is a little too faultily faultless, too icily regular for our taste. We need to spice it up with a small inexactness or two. It will become more beautiful if we depart a little from the norm.

So we take the standard nose and very slightly we lengthen it. Ah, that's better! Encouraged, we continue lengthening. And as we do so we find that beauty increases up to a maximum and thereafter declines. Beyond a certain length every fractional increase makes the face less attractive until it becomes positively ugly. Indeed ultimately it becomes so hideous that we recoil from it in horror. There is nothing intrinsically wrong with a six-inch nose; many creatures possess them. But on humans it is a large inexactness. And, because they break our laws of nature, large inexactnesses shake the foundations of our world as surely as does an earthquake. And they terrify us.

Let us look next at that other familiar source of visual beauty: landscape.

We can divide landscape into three categories according to the length of time we have known it. First the Wilderness – by which I mean those features that have remained more or less unchanged over thousands if not millions of years: sea, mountains, deserts, forests, wild plants and animals. Obviously European man, who has grown up in harmony with his sea coast, his mountains, his plants and his trees and who finds them still much as they were a hundred thousand years ago, will reserve for them his greatest affection.

Next comes the Cultivated Rural: fields, woods, paths, lanes, cottages and farms. Here there has been change but the change has been slow and has left much of the original wilderness untouched. An oak tree is still an oak tree whether growing wild in a forest or herded into a wood to be used as fuel. The Cultivated Rural was undoubtedly good, and although perhaps the straight lines of hedges may have seemed a little unnatural when they first appeared, we have accepted them now as part of what we call 'natural beauty'.

Lastly comes the Urban. Here changes are taking place very rapidly and little survives that is more than a hundred years old. Not surprisingly what is old – and what gave us the protection from weather and from marauders that we needed for our survival – we now look on as beautiful. But by today's standards it is no longer good. Equally, what is new – and what might or might not prove itself also to be good – has not had a chance yet to become beautiful. Just how we can attempt to fuse today's good with yesterday's beautiful is something I will consider in a moment. Let me start at the beginning: let me start with the Wilderness.

Once again we welcome small inexactnesses, small departures from the norm. We like to be able to predict, but a world without surprises would be a dull one indeed. And so we rejoice that the leaves on a tree are not all identical. This is possibly why, of all trees, I most love the oak in early summer. The leaves of other trees – beech, hazel, holly, for example – are almost indistinguishable one from another; they conform almost too exactly. There may be no single colour more lovely than that of beech leaves in May; but it is only a single colour, and you will walk through a beech forest in vain looking for another. But oaks vary so much that one can almost say it is the exception rather than the rule to find two exactly alike. Nor do they vary in just one respect. The leaves change colour as they open, so that the colour of a tree changes from day to day. Moreover, different trees go through different colour changes. Some produce a green that is very close to being a luminous yellow, almost dazzling, especially when seen against heavy storm clouds. Finally there are the even more lovely variations from leaf to leaf. This is most striking in the leaves that spring up round the base of a tree or round the stump of one that has been felled. To the varying shades of green are here added shades of bronze; and coupled with this are variations in shape and size, so that it is almost impossible to find two that are identical. Yet at the same time all this variety falls strictly within limits. An oak leaf is always recognizably an oak leaf.

This is the beauty of nature: the immense variety that it achieves while yet conforming sufficiently nearly to the rules. How dull if all primroses looked exactly alike. How pleasant it is to search for the biggest ones – and then perhaps to include in our bunch some that are small and neat and a few buds as well. How pleasant it is to sit beside the sea and watch the waves coming in, curling over, breaking and flinging themselves up the sand. How dull if they were all the same. How much more fascinating to watch for the one that is a little bigger (but only a *little* bigger) than its fellows and to follow its course as it moves towards the shore. There! That one! Will it break too soon and waste its energy? Will it collide with a retreating wave? Or will it rush up the sand and establish a new record?

And once again we recoil from the variation that is too great, from the freak, the monster, the deviant. The other day I cut a branch off the beautiful winter flowering prunus that grows on our bottom lawn. It was April. The young leaves were almost fully opened, and on this particular branch there were so many leaves, each one so beautiful. It should have been the most beautiful branch of the tree, it was so thick with beautiful leaves. But it wasn't. There were too many leaves. It was unnatural. It broke the rules by too great a margin. Something was wrong, though I didn't know what. I only knew it was ugly. I cut it off and took it to the bonfire. I didn't want to look at it.

We gaze at mountain scenery; we watch the waves breaking on the shore; we walk through a bluebell wood in May or a beech wood in October. And we are filled with a sense of beauty. We can feel it seething inside us. How do we react to it? Do we just return home feeling refreshed, like a thirsty man who has drunk a glass of water? Usually this is all that happens, but now and again we respond more actively. Richard Jefferies, as I have already said, used to lie down on the ground, prostrating himself, in order to feel the earth beneath him, feel it with the whole of his body; and he would hold things in his hand, grains of wheat, earth, stones, feeling them with his fingers. It was as if the sense of sight alone was too small a doorway for all the beauty that was pressing to get in and he had to open another – the sense of touch. Once my wife and I, walking among the hills in Italy, came suddenly upon a hollow that was purple with pansies. It was not enough to look at them. We had to sit among them and feel them and drink them in through our skin. Often in a wood or a meadow I feel this need to sit and then to stretch myself out on the ground and feel the ground with my hands, to explore it with my fingers. It might seem a little odd to come upon someone behaving in this way in a meadow; but it is, of course, how millions behave every summer on our beaches without any embarrassment.

Inland we prefer to be seen picking flowers – putting a sprig of heather in our buttonhole or gathering a bunch of primroses. My earliest memories of wild flowers are connected with primrose picking. 'Don't pick them, darling. Just look at them and then leave them for others to enjoy.' The young, environmentally conscious mother thinks she is offering sound advice. She is not! She is denying her child the opportunity of establishing what may well be one of its strongest links between past and future, of turning that vision of Heaven which is its birth-right into a memory that can be recalled and which will colour all future experience. Of course one should pick with consideration, leaving plenty for others to enjoy and plenty to seed for next year. But happily the commonest flowers, by their very commonness, have established in our eyes a beauty that is often lacking from rarer specimens; and primroses, daisies and buttercups will quickly replace the flower you take with another.

Clutched in a child's hand, warm and limp, the little harvest may not look very lovely, and a drink of water may never quite succeed in reviving it. But never mind. The picking was the pleasure – looking, finding, looking *closely* (so different from the casual glance we give as we pass by – like talking to a friend rather than nodding to an acquaintance) seeing how they grow, feeling along the stalk with the fingers, feeling where the eye cannot see, learning how best to snap the stalk, feeling it snap, smelling the flowers, arranging them in the hand, adding a leaf or two for variety . . . A blind child could pick primroses and get some of the pleasure I used to get. If I can still see those bunches I gathered, I can no less vividly feel the sensation in my finger tips as my hand went down into the cool depths and finger and thumb slid along the velvet stem and finger nail snapped it off.

We gather flowers and twigs and bear them home, but the fields and mountains and lakes we must leave behind. We can climb the mountain or swim in the lake or walk to the top of the hill or dip our toes in the stream. And thus we can acknowledge the beauty we find and take home with us the memory. But if we want something more tangible, we must be content with something smaller. So we build ourselves a garden and in it we have a rockery and a pond.

Though I suppose man's aim when he first built himself a garden was to possess his own supply of food plants, his later aim was to possess beauty. Initially the beauty he attempted to capture was the beauty of the Wilderness. But as he slowly tamed the Wilderness and found his work good, so a new beauty gradually established itself, the beauty of the Cultivated Rural; and this too he brought into his garden. He made himself a lawn and on it he built a rustic summerhouse with a winding path leading up to it. Finally the garden became its own source of beauty; and so the garden we make today captures the beauty we find in mountains and lakes, in fields and cottages and in other gardens.

Finally, and most important of all, we respond to beauty by arming ourselves with paints, paint brushes and an easel. For as artists we are able to satisfy not only our own need to possess beauty but also the needs of others. Through art we transmit experience.

There are, it seems to me, four distinct stages in the development of art.

The first stage is to copy as accurately as possible what the eye sees. Those beautifully painted flowers: you can almost smell them, they look so real! Those pictures of the sea, of bluebell woods and cottage gardens that we hang above our mantelpieces: how pleasant on a cold winter's evening to forget for a moment our drab urban surroundings and be transported to that little fishing village where the sun shone and everyone was so happy!

The second stage is to innovate, to move things around

– bring this tree forward and take away that one altogether. The artist, if not lord of the forest, is after all lord of his canvas. He can invent as well as copy.

The third stage is to emphasize. Anyone can see that the perfect daisy is a yellow circle inside a white circle. The circle is a very simple geometrical figure and most daisies depart from it only very slightly. But other patterns may be more complicated or more hidden or less commonly seen or the departure may be greater. We may know what the leaf of a beech tree looks like, for they are all much the same. But do we know how a beech tree holds its branches? Is there an underlying pattern here which is less obvious – one which perhaps distinguishes the beech from the oak or the elm? By finding it and then emphasizing it the artist can show us something that possibly on our own we had failed to notice.

The fourth and final stage in the development of art is to abstract the pattern and dispense with the tree. This is what we mean by 'abstract' art. The word, however, can be applied not just to pictures but to everything that man makes – his clothes, his utensils, his furniture, his houses, his machines, his towns and his factories. For just as a cook adds essences of this and that to improve the taste of his food, so does the craftsman add essences abstracted from the visual world to improve the appearance of his work. Such essences can be used either structurally or decoratively and they can be abstracted either from the natural world or from the work of previous craftsmen.

Thus a man looks at a tree, abstracts the cylinder and builds himself a stone pillar. Then he looks at the horns of a ram, abstracts the spiral and uses it to decorate the top, and so he achieves the Ionic column. But man the artist can only make suggestions. It is man the scientist who must take the decisions and do the actual building. Sometimes the builder welcomes the artist's advice; at other times not.

In this particular case, having completed half a dozen columns and wondering how to link them together, he turns, not to the artist but to the mathematician. And the mathematician hands him a triangle. The triangle is man's very own invention, possibly his greatest and, unlike the wheel, inspired by nothing that is to be found in nature. The builder places it on top of his columns and the job is done. The artist has reservations about the triangle: it is not what he would have advised. He would have preferred something a little more graceful, curved like the branch of a tree. However, it is undoubtedly good and so in time will seem beautiful. And when it does, men can forget trees and rams and Euclid and see instead a Greek temple with a beauty all its own ready to be abstracted and used in buildings all over Europe.

How nice if it were always like that! But alas it is not. Mankind is like a train. In the engine driver's cab sits the scientist armed with his triangles, doing his calculations. In the guard's van sits the artist with his pencil and paper, looking backwards out of his rear window and controlling the brakes. Once upon a time it was easy: there was no hurry. The artist drew his pictures, sent them up the corridor to the front where the scientist studied them and maybe used them. But then quite suddenly (if you think in spans of a thousand years, anything that has happened in the last few hundred will seem sudden) the scientist became impatient. Come along! Let's get moving! And he flung more coal on to his fire. The artist in his van was nearly thrown off his feet. The scenery went rushing by. It was extremely hard to draw anything when travelling so fast. Frantically he applied his brakes. Not only was it difficult to draw, but it was becoming increasingly difficult to get such pictures as he could produce through to the other end. And even when he succeeded, the scientist was more often than not too preoccupied even to glance at them. It was all very disheartening.

Eventually the inevitable happened. Somewhere around the time of the Industrial Revolution a coupling snapped. The front half of the train shot ahead even faster. To a bystander it might seem now to be completely out of control. But the scientist was perfectly happy. He was solving problem after problem. Each of his solutions seemed somehow to create yet another problem, and this was marvellous for it meant there was never an end to his work. Gradually the two halves of the train drew further and further apart, and as the rear half began to slow down, the artist resumed his work. There was not much point to it now: no one was particularly interested. So he doodled away for his own amusement; at least it gave him something to do.

Where will it all end? What will become of the train? Will it ever reach its destination?

Eventually the front half, unrestrained by the back, will go off the rails. We can only hope that this will be sooner rather than later and that the crash will not be totally disastrous.

Will the lesson have been learned? Will our appreciation of beauty be seen now for what it is, a gift the enjoyment of which should not be confined to an annual holiday by the seaside and an occasional visit to an art gallery? Will it become again and remain for ever more what it once was: a part of our everyday lives, the wisdom of the past offered to us, not as something to be learned the hard way with chastisement and tears, but as a pleasure as intense as anything we know? It is almost past belief that we ever chose to reject it.

If mankind is a train, so too is individual man. In each of us there is a scientist up in the front staring ahead and an artist in the tail looking behind. And in the middle there can be tension. But there need not be. We may despair for mankind as a whole but we need not despair for the individual. Our new towns may fall, if not to the barbarian from without, then to the vandal within. Our factories may spew out engines of destruction at one end and poisonous excreta at the other, and if we are not killed by the first we may die from the second. But never mind! While there are chisels to carve with, men will carve. While there are needles to sew with, women will sew. With our chisels and our needles, our pens and our brushes, our looms, our wheels and our lathes we will continue to record our love for the world.

The volcano will erupt and it will overwhelm us. But years later an archaeologist will dig down through layer upon layer of trash and at the bottom he will come upon a fragment of wood and a fragment of cloth.

And another renaissance will have begun.

6 *Morality and Law*

When we are hungry or in pain, we know it at once. Our body protests. And we have discovered various remedies – like eating something or rubbing the sore spot – to relieve the discomfort. So, whatever else man may be, he is, first of all, Solitary Man, attending to his own needs. After all, if he neglected himself he would die.

But if we have neighbours we soon discover something else: there are things they do that annoy us. We could suffer in silence of course, arguing perhaps that we all have a right to do as we please. But we prefer not to. Instead we make protesting noises. And they at times make protesting noises back at us. So our next discovery is that the hunger or pain felt by us can be felt equally by them. This sets us a problem, a problem familiar to every dog that confronts another across a bone, and one which, many thousand years after we first met it, we are still trying to solve.

But meanwhile our second discovery has led to a third. If two of us want the same thing and neither of us alone is able to get it, we can perhaps succeed if we combine our efforts; and then we can share the benefits. Thus Social Man is born, and the important thing to realize is that he is the product of Solitary Man. If Solitary Man had not first said, 'You are annoying me,' there could never have been Social Man to reply, 'Why, so I am. I'm terribly sorry.' If Solitary Man had not first said, 'I want this but alone I cannot get it,' there could never have been Social Man to say, 'I want it too. Let's get it together.' And we should not think the worse of Social Man if his respect for the rights of others and his offers of help spring initially from self-interest.

Though (in my model world) Social Man evolves from Solitary Man, he does not replace him. In every community both must survive. For there are certain things that men do best as a team and other things they do best as individuals. Furthermore, there will be moments in the course of each day when even the most social among us must pay attention to his own needs – even if only to eat and sleep. And there will be moments when even the most solitary will consider others – even if only to listen to what they are trying to say to him. And there will be moments when social and solitary are in conflict – even if only when we are too tired to listen properly.

I have said that in nature each species has its own ideal or perfect form, its scientific definition; and I said that each individual departs slightly from this definition, showing some small but welcome inexactness. It is as if each species has its particular target. Each individual then aims at the bull, misses but scores an inner. With humans it is different. We have not one but two perfect forms, perfect solitary and perfect social; and we aim at neither. Instead we join the two with a line. Each of us then chooses his own particular point on this line, makes that his bull, aims – and misses. Thus our combined shots do not form a circle round a point but a sort of sausage round a line, with perfect solitary lying just beyond one end and perfect social just beyond the other.

Towards one end of the sausage is Mainly-social Man, and one can picture him readily enough. He is the member of the chorus. He is one of the platoon of soldiers drilling on the parade ground. His individual identity is largely submerged in the identity of the group of which he is a member and on which he is dependent. Mainly-solitary

Man one perhaps thinks of as a recluse, living on his own. So he may be. But it is equally possible to be solitary in the presence of others. So he can be the soloist in the choir. He can even be the conductor of the orchestra, the sergeant in charge of the platoon. For Social Man needs Solitary Man to command him.

In an earlier chapter I argued that throughout our lives, from birth to death, we collect and store away the certainties of this world, the things that do not change or which change in a regular, predictable manner. If we were all mainly solitary we would treat other men rather as we treat wild animals. We would learn to distinguish the weak and harmless from the strong and fierce, chasing the one and avoiding the other. If we were mainly social our actions would be devoted to the well-being of others. In both cases in our encounters with our fellow men we would know with fair certainty how they were likely to behave towards us.

Instead, however, all of us being in differing degrees part solitary, part social, these near certainties have gone. This man, for instance, whom we have not seen before: will he help us or will he try to knock us on the head? How can we know? The answer is that we cannot unless we attempt to replace natural certainty by a sort of artificial certainty. This is what man has done. He has done it by means of boundaries and laws; and he is doing it all the time. Every community, whether primitive tribe, modern nation, trade union or local chess club, has first its boundary – which may be something physical on the ground or alternatively a list of members – and secondly its laws or rules or regulations. Never mind where the boundary runs, the important thing is that it should be clearly marked. Never mind what the law states, the important thing is that we should know it and be able to rely on its observance. Certainties are what we most need. Of course we can never get them, never even get the near-certainties of nature. For this is the one great difference between nature's laws and man's: the falling stone has no option. Man has.

Whatever the law states, man always has the option of disregarding it. You cannot prevent people from stealing merely by saying 'Thou shalt not steal.' In addition there must be a means of both catching and punishing the thief. You cannot entirely remove man's freedom of action; usually the most you can do is threaten him with likely consequences, leaving it to him to decide whether or not the risk is worth taking. So 'Thou shalt not steal' becomes in practice: 'If you steal and are caught, you will be put in the stocks.'

The stocks were a double deterrent. Not only must they have been quite uncomfortable on their own account, but in addition one had to put up with the rotten eggs and the abuse of bystanders – an experience not quickly forgotten.

Nor have we forgotten. Who among us today can claim that, in his long history, he has never broken any law, never been punished, never suffered eggs or abuse? Even in our own personal lives – those that began a few score years ago – there will be memories (many of them dating from childhood or schooldays) of occasions when it has been made very plain to us that we have misbehaved. We can still hear those voices, angry, threatening, accusing, scornful, mocking, sorrowful. We call it the 'voice of conscience'. We can still feel the pain of those judicial lashes and unjudicial eggs. We call it the 'pangs of guilt'.

In other words (or so I believe) those inner promptings that tell us that this is right and that is wrong have their origin in the inherited memories of past experience. Just as man's memories of his relationship with nature led to his appreciation of beauty and ugliness, so his memories of his relationship with his fellow men provide him with a natural ability to distinguish between good and evil, an ability upon which subsequent teaching can be based.

How simple life would be if our borders were inviolate. But alas they are not. Very few communities have lived their lives in total isolation from the rest of the world. Islanders, putting to sea in their boats, have encountered other islanders; and tribesmen, curious to learn what lay on the other side of the hill, have there met other tribesmen. Who were these others? Well, one thing was certain: they were 'not us'. And they have remained 'not us' to this day: 'outsiders'. Outside our boundaries. Outside our law. Consequently our relations with them have always been totally different from our relations with our fellow 'insiders'. Thus, for example, 'Thou shalt not steal', a common enough law within a community has seldom applied to the property of outsiders. 'Thou shalt not kill' has never been more than a purely local law condemning murder. Shooting arrows or firing guns at those who happen to live over the border has not been considered a sin.

But if this distinction that we make between the lives of our friends and the lives of our enemies may seem a little illogical when judged by God, it is not illogical when judged by nature. We live in a world in which all forms of life have advanced by means of immense over-production followed by immense wastage and leading to the survival of the fittest. Like it or not, high infant mortality – whether in the form of the seeds that fall on barren soil, caterpillars devoured by birds or the children of men that go to nourish the worms – is an essential part of a natural process. And it is not really surprising or particularly reprehensible that man should have adapted this natural process to his own ends. Nor is it surprising that in its adapted form it should have proved just as effective. War, in other words, is man's contribution to evolution. The strong have slain the weak and civilization has marched from battle to battle led by the armies of the conqueror.

Let us not feel too sorry for those who were killed: they would have died in any case, died in their youth. There was not room for them all. And so, if they had not been killed in battle, disease or starvation would have claimed them. War is neither wicked nor cruel, and this in our hearts we all know. Civilization has marched behind its victorious armies. Victory has generally brought to those who survived a fuller, richer life. And we are the sons and daughters of these survivors. Can we be blamed if we still worship what over the years has brought so many blessings? Whatever reason may now whisper in our ear, emotionally we remain warriors. Tiny children still play with their toy guns. Boys are still addicted to their war stories. Almost every display of communal unity is headed by marching troops. And old men, who might occasionally recall the dead bodies they had trodden on or tripped over in their youth, spend happy hours with their model soldiers on the dining-room floor fighting again the glorious battles of the past.

Thus, although in his behaviour towards his fellows, individual man is part solitary, part social, his communities in their behaviour towards each other are still almost wholly solitary.

Clearly, therefore, for a community to survive alongside others it needed to be strong and united. It needed Solitary Man to command it and perhaps a handful of other Solitaries to solve the various problems that confronted it. But for the most part its need was for Social Man – law-abiding citizens, disciplined troops, all putting the communal good above their own. Thus the law in its early days was concerned with what the individual should or should not do in the interests of society. Only very recently has it concerned itself with what society should or should not do in the interests of the individual.

One can picture a primitive tribe under its tribal leader and with the rudiments of tribal law and some means of law enforcement. An early discovery must have been that it was better when a law was obeyed willingly and gladly rather than reluctantly and under threat, that discipline imposed from above could be greatly helped when reinforced by loyalty from below rising up to meet it. And an early problem – one still with us – was the problem of succession. What happened when the old chief died? Even if his son inherited the power, did he always inherit the loyalty?

Loyalty was something one felt. It could not be imposed. Indeed one could not even impose it on oneself. It was like a plant with deep roots: once established it was not easy to move. And so, to survive, it needed to be rooted in something more permanent than individual human life. What?

Of the various answers that man has found the best is 'God'.

By 'God' I do not mean the Creator of the Universe. I mean the 'Tribal-Chief-who-does-not-die', that shadowy figure who stands just behind the current chief and who looks a little like his late father.

As a child and at school I was taught that 'God' was the Creator of the Universe and I was taught to think of this 'Creator' as a person, indeed as a man. 'He' and not 'She'. Now a 'person' to me was someone who, if he was here, was not simultaneously there. If he was like this, he was not simultaneously like that. If you wanted to speak to a person on the telephone you had to dial the right number. If by mistake you dialled the wrong number you got a different person. Moses and Isaac and Elijah and Peter and Paul had all, so I understood, dialled the right number. The Egyptians, the Philistines, the infidel and the heathen had dialled the wrong number and were speaking to false gods – 'gods' with a small 'g'. Later I was struck by the fact that the God of the Old Testament seemed to be very different from the God of the New. The one so cruel, so vindictive, smiting enemies left and right, the other so kind and loving: could they really be the *same* 'person'? Had Isaac after all got it wrong? Or had we all got it wrong? It was then that I read Winwood Reade's *The Martyrdom of Man* and saw 'God' not as the Creator of the Universe but as something man had invented, a series of portraits, an evolving idea. When I first met this definition I liked it so much that I discarded altogether the previous one. But many of our commoner words have more than one meaning, and 'God' – even with a capital 'G' – has at least three. It can be defined first as 'the Creator of the Universe' – a being that exists somewhere beyond the range of our telescopes and indeed (if we are honest) largely beyond the range of our comprehension. Its second definition might be 'God as perceived by individual man'; and its third definition might be 'God as presented to man by authority – the God of Religion'. Clearly the first definition is of something which, however nebulous to us, is absolute and unchanging. The second will differ from person to person, while the third, even within Christendom, will differ from age to age and community to community.

In this chapter it is only the third definition that I am interested in. We can compare the various evolving forms of 'God' to our various evolving pictures of the universe – Ptolemy's, Copernicus's, Newton's, Einstein's. We do not conclude from the fact that these are so contradictory that the universe itself does not exist. So if the 'God' (definition 3) of the early Christians differs from that of the early Israelites, this should neither surprise nor distress us. The one developed from the other. Each was appropriate to its time and place. And both today still have their relevance. And 'God' (definition 1) is quite unaffected.

But a puzzle still remained. I was happy with my own interpretations of the three definitions. I was happy that others should have different interpretations. What puzzled me was that they objected to or were in some way upset by mine. It didn't matter to me what they believed; so why did it matter to them what I believed?

I know the answer now. I had been misunderstanding the meaning of the word 'religion'.

To me 'religion' had meant 'the Christian religion' and this in its turn had meant a collection of 'beliefs' that told us about the origin of the world, about an event that had occurred 2,000 years ago and about man's ultimate destination. These were not topics that I pondered on very often or which seemed to me to affect my daily life very much, and so it seemed to me that whether I accepted or rejected them was very much my own affair and of no possible interest to others.

However, if one thinks of 'religion' not as man's answers to certain questions but as a means of forming and holding together a community, then things become clearer.

Though religion may today be about God, it started with that shadowy figure long ago who helped the current chief to rule and thus ensured the tribe's survival and so the survival of all its members.

One can picture them – dead father and living son – side by side, the father commanding the loyalty, the respect, the awe, while the son commanded the soldiery. How natural that over the years the father should develop an eye that could see into men's houses, into their very hearts. How natural that his son, unable to punish crimes he was not aware of, should make it known that punishment was only delayed. Yes, indeed the father, though dead, was well able to impose discipline as well as attract loyalty.

Eventually the son died, but the father lived on. There was no need for him to die. He was dead already and so immortal, the father of fathers, the chief of chiefs, God. Did he lead his armies into battle? Did he smite the outsider? Of course. Was he a tyrant, exulting in his power, proud, cruel, vengeful? Naturally.

Thus we can imagine him, thousands of years ago, the immortal head of hundreds upon hundreds of small communities scattered over the face of the world. Almost all these Gods are today forgotten. A mere handful survive – and one in particular. And if one wants to study the God-of-Religion, then undoubtedly the Old Testament provides the earliest, most fully documented starting place, and one, moreover, that leads directly and continuously to the God of Christianity today. To ignore the God of Isaac because he exhibits so many of the vices that today we condemn is as illogical as ignoring primitive art because the artist hadn't yet mastered the rules of perspective.

God and king had then and have still a common purpose: to unite the nation, to defend it against attack, to preserve its identity in adversity and, since this is in the nature of competitive man, to lead it to victory against its neighbours and so to extend its boundaries and increase its wealth. It is no condemnation of religion that religious wars are every bit as bloody as imperial wars. The 'Peace of God' is really no different from 'Pax Romana'. It may well be (I do not know) that Christ's unique relationship with God (definition 1) enabled him to show his followers a God of Love rather than a God of Fear, a single God caring for *all* mankind and not just the Hebrews. But to an outsider this God would appear to differ little from an Alexander or a Caesar, a conqueror building an empire, offering peace only to those who submitted . . . And so, although there was perhaps a moment when one of the duumvirate might have sheathed his sword or forged it into a ploughshare, the moment passed; and shortly afterwards priests were once again giving armies their blessing, assuring them that God was on their side and would grant them victory. And when new territories were acquired, the conquered were urged – not always too gently – to swear allegiance not only to the crown but also to the cross.

This duality between church and state explains why it once mattered so much what men believed. Their belief showed where their loyalties lay. Failure to bow down before God was equivalent to failure to stand up before the king. Both were punishable offences . . . and the memory still lingers to this day. At the back of many a Christian's mind the agnostic, whatever Christian virtues he may possess, is still a traitor. He is the insider who has gone over to the enemy. And this explains why to many Christians it *does* matter what their fellows believe.

I said in an earlier chapter that man's actions are governed partly by reason, partly by emotion. Reason argues from the files of experience collected and stored away during the individual's lifetime. Reasoning Man is therefore flexible. New experience added to the files may alter the argument. The discovery (for example) that something previously thought to be harmless is in fact dangerous will have an immediate effect on our actions. Emotion on the other hand argues from the files inherited at birth. These cannot be added to, though they can of course be disinterred and the dust can be blown off them. Emotional Man is therefore largely inflexible. If (for example) he is frightened of spiders he is likely to remain frightened of spiders even though reason assures him they are harmless.

What is true of individual man is true equally of his communities: these too are influenced by reason and emotion. And the most satisfactory arrangement – and the one we favour in the west – is for the state to govern largely through reason and the church through emotion. The state concerns itself with the more immediate problems confronting society, problems that may change from day to day and which therefore call for flexibility. Its laws require constant amendment. Yesterday (for example) we were allowed to drive our car down this road; today we are not; and reason, with luck, will accept the logic. The church on the other hand concerns itself with society's more general, fundamental and unchanging problems. Its laws are more rigid; and emotion accepts the validity of what for so long has been considered valid.

Because the state is flexible it will, if it is wise, allow its members to be flexible too. It will not only impose discipline but it will allow freedom and encourage initiative. The state needs both Social and Solitary Man. But the church, because of its very proper and necessary rigidity is concerned almost entirely with loyalty and conformity. It gives its blessing to Social Man. It mistrusts Solitary Man.

Earlier in this chapter I pictured man's communities as sausage-shaped, stretched between Perfect Social Man at one end and Perfect Solitary Man at the other. I chose the words 'Social' and 'Solitary' – borrowing them from the insect world – because I did not wish to imply judgment. Man, it seemed to me, displayed both characteristics. They were of equal value to him, and the inevitable interplay between them and between men who possessed them in different degrees was what made human life so varied and so exciting. The Christian church accepts these two poles but it labels them differently. 'Social' becomes 'Selfless', 'Solitary' becomes 'Selfish'; and its judgment between the two is delivered without compromise and with the utmost force it can command. The two poles become two pedestals and on these stand two figures. The one is Christ, the other is the Devil.

Like the word 'God', 'Christ' has three distinct meanings. There is the historical Christ, the man who – whatever happened before or after – lived and died in Palestine around two thousand years ago. Certain facts about his life have been recorded for us, though we cannot be entirely sure how accurately; and naturally there is a great deal we do not and will never know. Secondly there is our own personal Christ, the man we feel we know in our hearts and with whom many of us can converse. Thirdly, parallel with the God of Religion, is the Christ of Religion: Perfect Man. 'Gentle Jesus, meek and mild.' Never mind if these were not characteristics of the historical Christ. They were the virtues that Charles Wesley considered desirable in Social Man. Today we may rate other virtues more highly; and so the Christ (definition 3) who stands on the pedestal is not an unchanging figure. At one moment he may be dressed in rags, on his knees, submitting passively to the scourgings of his enemies; but at another he may appear as a soldier, sword in hand, fighting for all that is good and just and right. Is it wrong that the church should thus manipulate the historical Christ to suit its purpose, dressing him up now in these clothes, now in those? I don't think so. If Christ is to remain our hero he must have the virtues we currently admire. If we allow our artists to paint him, not as he actually looked (because no one knows) but as they like to imagine him, why should we not allow writers and preachers the same liberty? We need heroes to worship, paragons to emulate. Our hearts are not stirred by a mere code of conduct.

So on one pedestal stands Christ, the representative of all those qualities considered most desirable in a well-disciplined community. And on the other stands the Devil.

Poor Devil! He has fared badly. If we know little about the historical Christ we know less about the historical Devil. We meet him briefly in the Gospel of St Matthew, and I must admit that I find him a not unlikable person. He is clearly a Solitary – not in the least wicked. And he nicely displays those qualities that I described earlier as belonging to Solitary Man. He is the discoverer: he has discovered how to turn stones into bread. He is the inventor: he has invented a means of flying. And he is the leader: he is the ruler of a large kingdom. These are abilities possessed equally by the historical Christ, who was also a Solitary. However, if the Devil has been labelled wicked, he is in good company. For so too have we. All of us. We too are wicked. We too are sinners. We too are guilty.

If we compare the organization of the Christian church with the organization of the state we will find many similarities. But there is one great difference. The state, like the church, has its list of sins. But until the individual has been accused (and often not until he has also been found guilty) he is considered innocent. It is not assumed by the state that every child is born a thief and a murderer, but it *is* assumed by the church that every child is born a sinner, that is to say someone who has broken the law of God. This is the doctrine of Original Sin, and one that, viewed from outside the church, seems both mistaken and unfair. And since it is clearly one that helps the church to make converts, it is hard not to view it cynically. Much harm has been done by the over-zealous application of the twin doctrines of sin and redemption, as Christians as well as non-Christians recognize. On the other hand, one must allow that many people (whether or not the first seed of guilt was sown by the church) do consider themselves sinners, and are filled with self-hatred and suffer agonies of guilt and remorse – often for no apparently good reason. It is no use their fellow men forgiving them, for their consciences will not. So the church offers God's forgiveness, and the inner voices are silenced. And lest its members divide themselves into those who are convinced they have sinned and those who are no less convinced they have not, the church decrees that *all* are guilty, all are equal. For equality is one of the strongest constituents of the cement that binds man to man.

From his earliest tribal days man has been the victim of conflicting loyalties. What was 'good' and 'right' could always be interpreted in at least two ways – good for him on one hand, good for the tribe on the other. The tribe made its laws. King and God took joint command; and, provided there was not too much rivalry between them, their laws did not conflict. 'Loyalty', they could tell their subjects, had only one meaning: loyalty to the tribe, the state, the nation; and this was acceptable provided the nation remained fairly small. But king and God were ambitious and sought to extend their influence: and this was where the trouble started. The larger the community grew the less strongly did it cohere, and smaller communities then sprang up within it. Each of these communities defined its territory, laid down its own laws (which applied of course only to its own members) and arranged suitable penalties for those who broke them. Today each one of us is a member of a dozen or more communities, some small, some large, many of them overlapping and many of them in conflict; and we may find ourselves looking on our next-door neighbour as simultaneously an insider and an outsider. How now do we define 'loyalty'? For if we are loyal to the trade union that demands our membership we may be disloyal to the firm that employs us. How do we define 'selfishness'? Is the miner who comes out on strike selfless – because he is willing to suffer personal hardship for the benefit of his fellow miners – or selfish – because he deprives the rest of the country of badly needed coal? What is the 'right' thing for us to do? We can do no more (and probably no less) than weigh up the likely consequences of our possible actions and choose that course where the punishment is least severe. This may sound cowardly, but it is not. For the voice of conscience may be loud and imperious and the pain of disobeying it may be more unpleasant for us than any pain our fellow men can inflict. Today when our leaders lament our lack of patriotism or of faith, they must realize that our nation and our church are not the only communities to which we as individuals may feel we belong. Other loyalties may for one reason or another take preference. Possibly this may be no bad thing. For loyalty to a community, however desirable, breeds a feeling of separateness from those outside it, which is less desirable. If we want to feel ourselves citizens of the world, we cannot so easily feel ourselves British. Ideally we might wish to unite the world into a single entity, pulling down all barriers between nations and churches and installing a single government and a single religion. But in practice this is impossible, for no cement is strong enough to bind together, heart and head, a community so large and whose membership is so diverse. As the human race develops so there will always be changes in the pattern of our lives and in our groupings. Communities may grow but their cohesion will weaken. And then new communities will be formed. It is like throwing pebbles into a pond. The first pebbles cause ripples, circles spreading outwards from the centre. At first these circles are clearly seen but soon they meet and blend. Then other pebbles are thrown and new circles are formed and these too meet and blend. And we are like leaves on that pond tossed up and down by the ripples. 'Whither mankind?' we cry, feeling that we must have a destination, even though, as individuals, we are unlikely to survive to reach it. Nowhere. Just up and down.

The more complicated the pattern of ripples on the water, the more complicated our problems and the harder they will be to solve. Man is not 'wicked' in any universal sense; not even 'selfish'. He is merely human. And his problems will not be solved by his becoming 'good' in any universal sense; for there is seldom a perfect solution to any problem. How terrible if there were! How terrible if one day we invented a computer that could solve everything! No more problems. No more struggling. No more ups and downs. No more rivalry. No more success. Just endless perfection doled out by a machine. Fortunately there is not the smallest fear of such a fate.

Politicians, empire builders, moralists and philosophers may point to a light at the end of the tunnel, a goal for mankind, that final grouping of us all into an order so perfect and so satisfying that none will want to change it. My ambition for mankind is more modest: it is that wherever we go (and nothing will stop us from going somewhere) we do not totally destroy ourselves on the way. If by chance we fail in this, if by some mishap the human race totally extinguishes itself, it will not be on account of our wickedness but rather on account of our strength. Man today is too powerful: he can inflict too much damage.

I suggested in my last chapter that Rational Man could destroy civilization through a miscalculation in his use of science, and that it was up to Emotional Man to attempt to restrain him. I pictured mankind as a sort of runaway train with the scientist up in the engine driver's cab shovelling more and more coal on to the fire – faster, faster, faster – while in the rear coach was the artist frantically applying his brakes. In this chapter I see mankind as a sort of supertanker. Emotional Man is at the helm and down below in the engine room are his armies of stokers blindly toiling away. Up in the bows Rational Man is on look-out.

The voyage so far has been uneventful. In the open sea there was no hazard. The tanker could forge ahead on its steady course. But land is now in sight. There are reefs ahead. The look-out can see them and shouts a warning. But can the helmsman hear? And if he hears will he heed? And if he heeds can he alter course in time? Or will the momentum of the great vessel carry it on to destruction? Warfare, which has powered mankind for countless thousands of years, driving us from success to success, is now our enemy. We can slaughter thousands and still survive. We can even slaughter millions. But today at a single word of command millions upon millions can be killed – and this is too many. Emotional Man, inflexible, cannot easily change his ways. Warrior Man, who has achieved so much with the sword, will not happily discard it. Adventurous Man is not content with what he has but must always risk one more throw. And Man the Leader, however large his empire, will always be looking for new lands to conquer.

Perhaps we can do no more than put our fingers in our ears, wait for the bang, and hope that we – or at least someone – will survive it.

7 *Love, Faith and Hope*

In the last chapter I examined the way in which communities, beginning with the tribe and progressing to the nation, have held themselves together. At all stages they have had a leader who has imposed his authority by means of power. There have not been many communities in the west that have survived in competition with their rivals without some form of leadership and some form of discipline. As the community grew in size so the structure of control became more complicated, and ultimately a hierarchy developed, a pyramid of authority. Above this pyramid, reinforcing the authority of the leader, hovered something that we call 'God'.

You can look at a pyramid from two opposite points of view: from the top downwards or from the bottom upwards. In the last chapter I was looking from the top and what I saw was discipline and the God of Authority. In this chapter I shall be looking from the bottom and I shall see loyalty and the God of Love. Religion viewed from the top offers the ruler a means of controlling the ruled. Viewed from the bottom it offers individual man a means of expressing his feelings about his fellow men, about the world and about himself. Love, faith and hope. I will start with love.

When man meets man, as when dog meets dog, the first question to be resolved is: 'Friend or foe?' In the western world the universal language for transmitting the message,

'I am a friend', is the smile. This is a visual message, one directed to the eye. But since smiles were not always easy to see, especially when coming from behind a beard, and since there was always the risk that one might be directing one's smile towards someone who was not going to return it, other visual messages were devised to indicate one's allegiance. And at one time or another men have sported red roses, red shirts, red ties, green berets and black bowlers. Their emblems have ranged from the smallest badge concealed behind the lapel of the coat to the complete outfit of the soldier or the footballer, from the woad of the ancient Briton to the latest fashion in eye shadow. And these have been worn not just for the purpose of identification but also with pride. How proud I was of the red cap I put on my head at the age of eight: I was now a schoolboy among fellow schoolboys. How proud I was of the battledress I put on at the age of twenty: I was now a soldier among fellow soldiers.

However, though man's allegiance is best established through the sense of sight, it is, as I said earlier, through the sense of sound that nearly all subsequent messages are passed.

Our first and most primitive form of language was, I suspect, a throat language, one made among our vocal chords and resembling the noises made by mammals generally. Later we developed a second language, one made in the mouth with tongue and lips. This second language was quite distinct from the first, greatly superior to it and eventually superseded it. But the first language nevertheless survived, for it had two important advantages. The first was its greater carrying power, making it particularly suitable for communicating at a distance to a number of people. The second was that it could be reproduced artificially. So the two languages went their separate ways. The new one, because of its flexibility, was used to convey man's most up-to-date messages and became the language of speech. The older one remained the vehicle for his more basic messages, his emotions, and became the language of music.

Because of its carrying power music was particularly suitable for conveying those emotions that link men together into communities. Of the many forms we have today one can guess at the three earliest. First: the summoning music, whose message is quite simply 'Come here'. It survives today in bugle call and church bell. Next: the get-together music, music designed to introduce individuals to each other so that they interact in a friendly, happy way. This is the dance. Last: the work-together music, music designed to get the group, whose members are now on good terms with each other, to act in unison in order to perform some particular task. The most familiar form of this is the march.

In both dance and march we carry out certain movements which need to be coordinated. Left, right, left. We must all be in step, which means we must all know a little in advance how the music is going to direct our legs. We must be able to predict. And so the music must form a recognizable pattern of sound, a repeating pattern. In other words, it must possess rhythm.

Today we still march and dance; and sometimes the music is provided artificially by others and sometimes naturally by ourselves. When the regimental band is silent soldiers will sing as they march along the road. Sailors go 'yo-heave-ho' as they haul on the rope. However, in the western world much of our best music now calls for no response at all on our part. We listen in silence and stillness. But we do so only out of consideration for our neighbours. Inside ourselves we are still responding as it was intended we should. We are shouting and stamping and waving our arms; and sometimes we can barely restrain a nod of the head, a laugh or a tear.

I have said that the difference between reason and emotion is that reason, being based on the collection of experiences that we have accumulated in the course of our personal lives, is flexible, readily adapting itself to new experiences, whereas emotion, based on a resumé of inherited experience, is not. It follows from this that speech, continually adapting itself to keep pace with reason, is something we have to learn; and we continue learning throughout our lives as new words are added to our vocabulary. Also, since men in different places will adapt their speech differently, different countries will have different languages. Music, on the other hand, being the language of emotion, changes less. The young child has to be taught the meaning of 'Mummy' and 'Daddy', but immediately and instinctively he understands a simple tune. Also, since our emotions have their origins deep in our past and since our past spreads out like the roots of a tree to cover a very wide geographical area, it is not surprising that music is a much more universal language and that national variations are much smaller. If I cross the Channel I have a struggle to understand what the French are saying to me, but their music speaks to me so plainly that I can scarcely detect even a foreign accent.

Except for bells and bugle calls, music, the language of emotion, speaks solely to our emotions. If we are drawn to music, if we enjoy listening to it, it is because of its emotional appeal. We do not feel obliged to offer a rational explanation. We do not excuse half an hour spent listening to Beethoven by pretending that we were making a study of harmonics. With speech it is different; for speech is a double langauge, capable of expressing both reason and emotion. It can be mainly the one or mainly the other or a bit of both. Thus the instructions that accompany some new gadget may appeal solely to reason and will be 'true' if, by following them, we are able to get the gadget to work; while a poem may appeal solely to emotion, being 'true' only to the extent that we find it moving. These two forms of truth can lead to confusion. A story, for example, can be presented in such skilful language that we not only accept it as emotionally true but find it hard not to believe that it is rationally, literally, true as well.

Now I said in a previous chapter that man's relationship with the world around him, a world he perceived mainly through the sense of sight, gave birth to an emotion which, in a single word, one can call beauty. Parallel with this is man's relationship with his fellow men, perceived mainly through the sense of sound, giving birth to an emotion which, again to choose a single word, I will call love. This emotion he can express and transmit through music and speech. (Perhaps in parenthesis I should add that he can also express it visually through art, but that because human relationships are fluid and changing, art is rather too static for this purpose.)

Love takes various forms and these fall into two distinct groups. The first is what might be called family love: the love of a child for its mother, of a parent for a child, of man for woman and the love that links two friends. The second is community love: our feelings for our fellow men in general and the feeling we direct towards our leaders. As with beauty, so with love: we look for ways of expressing and enjoying it. We read exciting or romantic stories. We listen to music. We go to parties and dances and football matches. We spend our holidays on overcrowded beaches. Mainly-social Man likes large crowds. Mainly-solitary Man, unless he is the person the crowds have come to see, prefers his human company in smaller quantities.

Although authority may have something to say about family love, it is more concerned to stimulate community love: for this is what will hold a community together. Thus most children are encouraged to feel a certain pride in their school and a certain respect for their teachers. We learn to 'play up, play up and play the game', and the captain of the first eleven becomes our hero. The same thing may be observed in a nation. National pride is encouraged. And since it is recognized that less than half of us are likely to feel much affection for the current prime minister, we are offered instead the monarch as an individual upon whom we can focus our feelings of national loyalty. The Queen is thus two people. She is (as women's magazines are never tired of pointing out) 'Just like you and me' and in this role is allowed to choose her own hat. She is also a royal and must occasionally wear a crown. It could be said that when she puts on her crown she is no longer a human being but a figurehead. Maybe. But most emphatically she is no *mere* figurehead. The role she plays may have no rational validity – she makes no laws and commands no troops – but it satisfies an immensely strong emotional need, as can be seen in the crowds that gather outside Buckingham Palace waiting for that brief, distant appearance on the balcony. You may compare this to the crowds that gather at a folk festival hoping for a glimpse of a favourite singer; and of course the emotions are the same.

In the west we have two separate forms of government, a rational one and an emotional one: state and church. Let me now turn to the church.

I have already dealt with the disciplinary aspect of the church and I have said that discipline imposed from above is more effective if it can be reinforced by loyalty rising up from the bottom. This loyalty is one of the forms of love. In the state it is the emotion we direct towards the Queen. In the church it is the emotion we direct towards God.

I have said that the word 'God' can have three different

meanings. I am now concerned with definition 2: our own personal vision of God as opposed to the definition offered to us by authority.

'God the Father', 'King of Kings and Lord of Lords': so many of the words we use bring before our eyes a vaguely patriarchal figure. Suppose for a moment that God were presented to us not as man-shaped, not as a 'Father' or a 'Lord' but as something totally different – a vast, Divine Computer, for instance, or maybe something that cannot be visualized at all, like 'the ground of our being'. Can there be any doubt about the emotional loss? It is as if the royal family were to abdicate and we were offered in their place the crown jewels.

Again, if religion were concerned to offer us only a first cause, the Creator of the Universe, there would be no particular value in the idea of the Trinity. But if we think of God the Father as the being towards whom we can direct those feelings of devotion, admiration, awe and trust that man has always felt for the best of his leaders, then there is an obvious role for God the Son and God the Holy Ghost. There is no mystery here. If God the Father is our commander-in-chief, then God the Son is the fellow soldier who earns the posthumous VC, and the fellowship of the Holy Ghost is the sense of comradeship that permeates a body of troops on the battlefield. If God is headmaster, then Christ is head boy and the Holy Ghost the school spirit. Love, as I said, takes various forms. Here directed upon the Trinity are three of them. And the Virgin Mary and Christ Child provide us with two more.

Central to Christianity is a statement that I once found puzzling. It is that God so loved the world that he sent down from Heaven his only son to die for us that we should be saved. If we think of God as the all-powerful creator of the universe, this statement is meaningless. Such gods cannot experience suffering or make sacrifices or know death. Such gods are immortal. But if for God the Creator we substitute a picture of God the King, then indeed we have a truth. For the picture of a king whose devotion to the well-being of his subjects is so great that he is willing to sacrifice for them his most precious possession is one that arouses the most powerful emotion. And since this emotion is intensified if we can identify ourselves with those subjects, we are told that Christ died not just for the sake of some people living in Palestine two thousand years ago. He died for *us*.

Am I therefore suggesting that God and Christ are two fictional beings, no more real than King Arthur and Sir Lancelot? No, because to put it like that is to misunderstand how we understand things.

I said, when considering scientific law, that in order to understand (for example) planetary motion, we construct a model. We can if we like make an actual model, a planetarium, or we can make an imaginary model, such as Newton's world of forces and particles. If, for certain purposes, it is helpful to consider Uranus as a particle, this does not imply that Uranus *is* a particle. Nor does it imply that its motion round the sun is the only thing about it that can interest us. We might in addition like to investigate its chemical composition. Here Newton's model is no help at all.

In a similar way man tries to understand God. And one of his models, helping him towards an understanding of one of God's aspects, is the human family. This model is partly real, partly imaginary. Christ and Mary were real people; God and the Holy Ghost are perhaps rather less real. A degree of reality makes the model appear more convincing and therefore truer, but does not necessarily add to its value.

It is easy for the astronomer to appreciate the differences between the Uranus that is 'out there in the sky', the little blob of metal that represents Uranus in his planetarium and the pencil dot that represents the particle that represents Uranus on his sheet of paper. But general agreement is less easy when we try to separate the real from the imaginary, the actual from the model, in the contemplation of the God of Love. This is partly because love is an emotion and partly because God is invisible.

So some will claim that the Trinity is real; others will see it as a model that enables us to understand something that is real, arguing that we can never understand actuality except through models.

Just as its motion is only one of the aspects of a planet that we might wish to contemplate, so love is only one of the aspects of God. Another is faith.

Our life, as I have said, is built on certainties. If such-and-such happens, so-and-so follows. If I look at my watch I will know the time. This particular certainty saves me an immense amount of trouble and I have organized my life around it, so that if my watch suddenly misinforms me I am thrown into confusion.

If I do not have a watch, then perhaps I ask a friend and perhaps I have come to rely on that friend to tell me the right time whenever I need to know. So if suddenly my friend misinforms me, again I am thrown into confusion. In both cases the confusion is very much worse if I now fear that what has happened once is likely to happen again, if I have now lost confidence in my watch or my friend. Reason may well reassure me. My watch failed because I had forgotten to wind it up; my friend misheard my question: neither mishap need ever recur. But faith is an emotion and does not listen to reason. Like love it is something we *feel*. Without this feeling of faith – faith in the ordered running of the world, faith in other people, faith in ourselves – we could scarcely survive. Lacking all confidence in the successful outcome of any action, we would take no action at all. We would become mentally paralysed. And so whatever happens, faith must be kept alive. Whatever and whoever fails us, there must always remain something or someone who can be relied upon never to fail us.

This is what Christianity offers us: one absolute certainty. Faith in God. Trust in the Lord. Just as the God of Love – whatever mental picture we might choose to accompany those words – was the rallying point for our feelings of love, so faith in God – whatever exactly we expect of God in return for our faith – is the rallying point for our feelings of confidence.

I am writing these words not long after the earthquake in southern Italy. Entire villages were almost completely destroyed. There can be no disaster more calculated to shake man's confidence in the stability of his world than one which literally shakes the very foundations of that world, the solid rock beneath his feet. With every building a ruin, where did the villagers start their work of reconstruction? What particular need was the most pressing? According to reports they started with their church. I can only guess why; and I guess that, before any other task could be contemplated, they needed first to restore their shattered faith, their faith in God, their faith that it was still possible to lay stone upon stone.

A third aspect of God is hope.

Where faith is built on certainties, hope is built on uncertainties. Where faith can and should be immortal, hope comes and goes, surviving only so long as the object of our hopes lies in the future. Success as well as failure brings that particular hope to an end. We cannot live without faith. We can live without hope, but our lives would be plodding and sad. Hope is an emotion that man needs in order to make the best of his life, and like all beneficial emotions it is accompanied by great happiness. If hopes begin to fail us we are in danger of losing all feelings of hopefulness. Hope turns to despair. And so, however seemingly hopeless our lives, there must remain always something to hope for, some goal that will assuredly be ours one day, always within sight, yet always just out of reach.

This too is what Christianity offers us: one certain hope. Heaven.

Love, faith and hope. St Paul's famous trio, three of our most precious emotions and three that are the special concern of the Christian church. Let me now stop being general and become more personal. Though we can perhaps argue someone into accepting a rational truth, we cannot argue anyone into accepting an emotional truth; for here each of us is unique. Our needs and our responses differ from person to person. So it is not man's perversity but rather his diversity that prevents us all from accepting the love, the faith and the hope that Christianity offers us. Here is how it is with me.

I said in my last chapter that each of us blends the social with the solitary in his own unique proportions. With me the balance lies heavily with the solitary. I was conscious of this as a child when I played frequently and happily alone. I was conscious of it as a schoolboy when I found it not easy to mix with other boys. I was conscious of it in the army when I did not specially need the comradeship of my fellow soldiers. And I am conscious of it today in my preference for rural rather than urban surroundings, working for myself rather than for an employer, and not greatly enjoying parties, reunions, societies or indeed any form of community life.

I can think of only one exception to this solitariness, one occasion only when I have experienced quite strongly the thrill of being in a crowd. This crowd was my division during the war – 56 Division – and the thrill was at its strongest when I was most aware of the division as a single entity. These occasions stand out vividly in my memory: in 1942 when we marched through Liverpool to the docks to embark on our troopships; in 1943 when we crossed three thousand miles of desert from Iraq to Tunisia – surely the longest caravan ever to have travelled that immense journey; again in 1943 when we sailed in a convoy of landing craft from Tripoli to Salerno; and finally on various occasions in Italy when we moved up for the big attack or flooded through for the big advance.

This feeling of being a part of something immeasurably larger than myself is the nearest that I have ever come to experiencing the love that Christianity offers – love directed upwards towards God and outwards towards our fellow men. But though the emotion was immensely sustaining at the time and though I treasure the memory, it is not an experience I have wished could be repeated. And in any case I do not think the church, even if I were willing to let it try, could ever rekindle a fire that is now burnt out.

Today my general (as opposed to specific) emotion of love is directed not towards humanity but towards all creation. My feelings are those of Richard Jefferies: an intense and burning love of the natural world – trees, flowers, hills, streams, meadows, footpaths, sea and shore, birds and insects, moon and stars, wind and rain, yes, even those arid deserts of the Middle East that I met as a young soldier. Jefferies focussed his feelings upon the sun; but though a community needs a focus or figurehead or rallying point for their emotions, an individual does not; and I have none.

As for my need for faith, this, too, I find rather in things than in people. In the war, when so much that seemed solid and enduring was being destroyed, I found it in the indestructible mountains of Italy and in the enduring countryside. I find it in the things of the past and the feeling that I belong to the past, am rooted in it, almost physically rooted in the solid ground beneath my feet. I find it in what, in a previous chapter, I called the Wilderness and the Cultivated Rural. It is exemplified by Hardy's poem, 'In Time of "The Breaking of Nations" ':

> . . . Only thin smoke without flame
> From a heap of couch-grass;
> Yet this will go onward the same
> Though Dynasties pass. . . .

This, of course, is what rural life has to offer. Urban life, unless in a very old town, seems transitory, artificial, superficial. We are separated from the ground by a layer of concrete and from the sky by the intervening rooftops. But in the country, hills and valleys are unchanging and the lane still follows the ancient track that men have walked for a thousand years. And each year the seasons return. We may lose faith in mankind but we can never lose faith in the opening bud or the falling leaf.

Finally, hope. There were moments at the beginning of the war when I was convinced that I would not survive it – and I didn't greatly care. There were moments later, in Italy, when the immediate prospect was so daunting that I could set my hopes no further away than the next half hour. But subsequently I have always found plenty to hope for. Some of these hopes may be only a few minutes away; others perhaps a day or two; few more than a year. Only once have I lifted my eyes to scan the distant horizon and wonder what lay over the edge. This too during the war; and what I was offered and what my heart went out to was Winwood Reade's vision of Perfect Man, of a Heaven set not in some other world but in this world. This particular Heaven satisfied me for many years. Today, however, I fear it can never be reached and that we are not even making much progress towards it. At the same time I find myself wondering if in fact such a Heaven would have much to offer to those who finally arrived there. Perfection is a little like an everlasting flower that never fades or drops its petals. And so my feelings here are crystallized by Tennyson's 'Ulysses'. Whatever may happen to mankind, for individual man there always:

> Gleams that untravell'd world, whose margin fades
> For ever and for ever . . .
> Death closes all: but something ere the end,
> Some work of noble note, may yet be done . . .
> . . . my purpose holds
> To sail beyond the sunset, and the baths
> Of all the western stars, until I die . . .

Nevertheless, if the Christian church cannot offer me love or faith or hope in the form that suits me best, this does not leave me indifferent to the life and teaching of Christ.

This is how I see it.

If we wish to communicate an emotion we can use our emotional language, music. A commander wishing his soldiers to feel brave gets the regimental band to play them something suitably martial. Alternatively we can use our rational language, speech, and arouse similar feelings with stories of valorous deeds.

The important difference between the two is that speech, unlike music, must be specific. That is to say you cannot arouse feelings of courage or of love, of excitement or of fear, by writing an essay on the subject but only by telling a story about particular people doing particular things.

These people need not be real people. Whether our

emotions were being stirred by Greek drama, medieval folk tales, Victorian romances or modern adventure stories, we have never demanded factual truth – and indeed we have seldom been given it. We have, however, demanded something else. Just as we need to know the laws that govern our own everyday world, so we need to know the – possibly very different – laws that govern the world in which our story is set, and in particular the extent to which that world matches up with the real world. We can accept any level of reality. What we cannot accept is any unexpected lowering of that level. Should that happen our faith in our imaginary world is shaken in the same way that faith in the real world is shaken when one of our established certainties fails us.

I remember a children's story I once read. From the way it started I assumed that, although it was naturally about fictitious children, its setting was real; and I adjusted myself to this level. Then, around Chapter Three, something unreal happened – some piece of magic – and at once, for me, the reality of the story was shattered and I could read no further. It was not that I disliked magic, but rather that magic, introduced into what I had assumed was an unmagic world, broke faith with reality. Even fantasy must establish and maintain its level of reality. Mr Toad can row a boat and drive a car. He cannot sprout wings and fly. He can disguise himself as a washerwoman well enough to fool a few unobservant humans. He cannot turn himself into a washerwoman.

Our stories range from the completest fantasy to the strictest truth. Truth is not necessarily more potent than fiction. Both have the power to move us. All we need to know is where within this range each particular story lies.

Herein is both the strength and the weakness of Christianity. It is based on the Bible and the Bible is based on fact. The strength is obvious: the people described are real people; the events described really happened. This gives the story an added truth, a factual truth, that degree of truthfulness that for some people (but by no means for all) lifts the biography above the novel. The weakness comes when we ask, 'But did it really happen exactly like this?' It is not Emotional Man who asks this question. It is Rational Man. For, having studied the events recorded and having compared them with what he knows of the real world, he finds inconsistencies.

Now it is bad enough when our faith in any story is shaken. It is worse when that story has been presented to us as historically true, for it then throws doubt upon historians. And it is infinitely worse if we have been led to believe that the book's author is God himself, the most utterly trustworthy Being in the world. For if God cannot be trusted to tell us 'the truth', then indeed no earthquake can more disastrously shatter our faith in life.

I put the word 'truth' in inverted commas because it is we, not God, who are defining it; and we do not all define it alike. Most people accept that the Bible is based on historical reality. But we do not all of us demand or expect the same degree of accuracy. The important thing for each of us is not the level of truthfulness that we have decided upon but that we should not lose confidence in this level and be compelled to lower it. Thus, for example, for those who regarded the story of creation as a scientifically accurate account of the origin of the world, the theory of evolution came as a serious blow to biblical truth. Today, however, we prefer to see Genesis as an early attempt to describe the world's beginning comparable to the astronomical theories of Hipparchus. Our faith in the Bible is no more shaken by the inaccuracies of the ancient Hebrews than is our faith in ancient Greece, in Socrates or Plato or the Parthenon shaken because Hipparchus thought the sun moved round the earth.

Today what worries us is not the truth of Genesis but the

truth concerning the life of Christ and in particular the circumstances surrounding his birth and death. It is of course Rational Man within us who worries, not Emotional Man. Rational Man doesn't like miracles. Again it is a matter of level. We have no need to believe that Christ was born of a virgin. We can quite well accept that this was just one of the stories that grew up about him after his death. He was, after all, no ordinary man, and in those days it was considered natural that extraordinary events should be associated with extraordinary people. The gulf that modern science has now set between the possible and the impossible did not then exist. Two thousand years ago the gospel story could be accepted without reservation. Two hundred years ago it could still be accepted. But today Rational Man is unhappy and would prefer a lower level of truth. Whether he can make the adjustment depends entirely on the reaction of Emotional Man. Like every schoolboy in those days I was taught and accepted that the gospel story – angels and all – was 'gospel truth'. Later I began to have doubts. Emotionally I was reluctant to give ground. There was something of an inner battle, though not a very painful one, and, as I said earlier, reason emerged triumphant. Subsequently I established a new level of truth and all was well. With others the battle is fiercer. Neither side is willing to give in, and in the end a curious compromise is reached. A bridge is built to span the gap between the two. This bridge is known as 'faith'.

It is confusing that the word is the same as the word I have been using to describe one of the aspects of God, for its meaning is different. The 'faith' we have in God is the faith that, acting on our emotions, conquers irrational fears, while the 'faith' we need in order to 'believe' is the faith that, acting on reason, silences rational doubts. This second form of faith may well bring to a happy end the most agonizing of inner conflicts, and so to many a convert it is seen as Christianity's most essential and wonderful ingredient. But of course where there was never a battle or where the issue was settled on reason's terms, there is no gap to close and no bridge is needed.

Let me illustrate what seems to me the essential difference between Christian and humanist.

There was a man who, having read about the Good Samaritan in Luke's Gospel, believed this story to be true in all respects. He knew the road that winds down through the mountains from Jerusalem to Jericho. It was indeed a road where robbers might lurk. And he had always assumed that the rest of the story was no less true, that the Samaritan was a real person, someone perhaps known to Jesus, just possibly even Jesus himself. And so it came as a great shock to him when a friend told him that it was 'only a parable'.

'Not true?' he cried in horror. 'Just a fairy tale – and the Good Samaritan no more real than Father Christmas? Don't be absurd!'

But his friend was adamant.

'It's you who are being absurd,' he said. 'Everyone knows it's a parable and that a parable is an *imaginary* story. Jesus was simply illustrating who was his "neighbour".'

The first man was extremely unhappy at these words, for they seemed to challenge all he believed in, his entire faith. What was worse, they threw doubt on Jesus's own veracity.

'You are quite mistaken,' he said, 'and I can prove it. Either Jesus was telling the truth or he wasn't: it's as simple as that. If he wasn't, he was lying. Are you saying that Jesus is a liar?'

Let us leave the two of them arguing and try to understand what they are arguing about; and let me start with that 'proof'.

It is of course fallacious, but it is worth looking to see exactly why. It is a proof borrowed from mathematics and one much used by Euclid in his geometry. It is known as *reductio ad absurdum*: that is to say you prove a thing by showing that all the other alternatives are absurd. The vital word here is 'all'. It is not enough to consider only *some* of the alternatives. In the precise world of mathematics we may well be confident that no other possibility has been overlooked; but the real world is less precise. Thus we may be tempted to base an argument on something Christ said. But can we be sure he used those exact words? Can we be sure of his exact meaning? Can we be sure he was correctly understood by his hearers and that they correctly reported what they had heard to people who correctly remembered it and later correctly recorded it? How easy it is – as we all know – to misunderstand and to misreport!

Alas for such proofs! They are worthless!

But did it in fact matter that the two men attributed different levels of factual truth to the story? Of course it mattered very much when the higher level was challenged; for no doubt the first man had built a whole edifice of philosophy, dogma and ritual on his assumptions. All this was now threatened and had to be defended. Yet if the two could stop arguing they would probably both agree that the purpose of Christ's story was to illustrate something in human nature – how humans feel towards each other – and to persuade his listeners that one way was better than another, to arouse their sympathies, to stir their emotions. It was not the factual truth of the story that mattered. It was its emotional truth.

This is how I feel about the whole of the gospel story. For me it is a parable, a single, vast parable. It is based on much that is factually true but it doubtless includes much that was embroidered upon as the reports travelled from person to person. And maybe it includes not a little pure fantasy. The whole forms one of the most moving stories the world has known; and it is one directed straight at our hearts.

So it is sad that Christian and humanist should argue about an aspect of it which, viewed from a suitable distance, seems not in the least important. It does the Christian case no good to offer a pseudo-mathematical proof of Christ's divinity. Nor does it help to bring the two sides together when the Christian equates 'belief' (by which he means no more than his chosen level of reality) with all that is best in human conduct.

I said in my last chapter that every community needs to establish its boundary and its laws. The Christian community is no exception. Certainly when it was fighting for its existence it needed to know friend from foe. Certainly it needed discipline within its ranks. 'Onward, Christian soldiers.' But is it quite like this today? Must the battle continue? To the outsider it may seem that the more important of the Christian laws govern his own life too; while those he cannot accept are of lesser importance, are less fundamental to human behaviour or more arbitrary – like the colour of the uniform worn by the soldier. It may seem to him too that Christ's message, his philosophy, the parable of his life, is for all men, believer and unbeliever, Christian and humanist alike.

So whatever barriers the Christian puts up – and indeed must put up – to keep the outsiders outside and the faithful faithful, there will be many on the outside who will look over the wall and say, 'Christ speaks for me too.' It is not only the Christian who can declare 'Jesus lives!' – as if he were saying something anyone might doubt. Of course he lives! Who looking around can possibly doubt it? All around us we have records of men and women who have spoken, written, painted, built, composed music, behaved towards their fellow men, fought battles and faced death, inspired by his story. Art, architecture, literature, music, human conduct: in so many of the fields of human endeavour do we see his presence and his influence alive today. How more than that can a person be said to 'live'?

In one field only is his presence most noticeably missing: science. Indeed, if we are to be honest, we would have to admit that science has, if anything, been impeded by Christianity. And this only confirms what I have said: that the important truth about Christ is not scientific, not rational, not historical, not factual, but emotional. If we were historians, concerned only to dig out the factual truth of exactly what did occur at the time of Christ's birth and death, we might well feel that the evidence at our disposal was scanty and untrustworthy. But we are not historians. If we wish to make up our minds on this matter, we may do so. We may interpret what we have read in any way we like. But having reached our own decision, let us realize that others may decide differently and that this is perfectly admissible and quite unimportant; and let us then seize upon those essential truths that we can all share. And let us, as equals, share them.

8 Towards a New Religion

Although I was born in London and spent my very early childhood there I have never felt myself to be a Londoner. Indeed at school I was deeply ashamed of my urban origins and envied those boys who had been born as well as bred in the country. In self-defence I would claim that I too was partly country-bred; for although my family still lived mainly in London, when I was five my father had bought a cottage in Sussex which we would visit every weekend and where I would spend the whole of my Easter and summer holidays.

These early feelings have never changed. Our present house is in the country. We moved here from the edge of Dartmouth some fifteen years ago. We moved to the edge of Dartmouth from the town centre ten years before that and to Dartmouth from London five years earlier. We had started in London after the war for no better reason than that it was generally assumed that if one sought fame and fortune this was where it was to be found.

So once again I am back in the country and more convinced than ever that this is where I belong; and although I am half a century older I still feel that thrill of pride at being able to call myself a countryman that I so vividly remember feeling when first we took possession of Cotchford Farm in 1925. I still feel as I felt then, not just that I am more fortunate than those who are compelled to live in towns, but that I am – in a way I cannot easily define

– superior to them. Just as the city man so often looks down on 'the provinces' where his 'country cousins' live, so I look down on the city man, unable to drive his smart car along our Devon lanes, unable to walk through our Devon mud, not knowing a buzzard from a crow or a celandine from a buttercup, lonely and bored – poor fellow – without his gay lights and urban bustle.

Even to our Dartmouth friends Embridge, though admittedly a very beautiful and peaceful spot, seems remote and isolated. They wouldn't choose to live here, not all the year round. This is understandable. Men are, after all, gregarious creatures, and villages and towns and cities are where their colonies are mostly to be found. If in the past there was an isolated house it was almost certainly inhabited by someone who needed to live in that particular place because that was where he worked – because he was a farmer or a forester or a miller.

Today, however, it is possible to live in one place and work in another and so these isolated rural houses are now frequently occupied by people who, having a choice, prefer such surroundings. Why do we have this preference? Partly it may be a love of solitude. Partly it may be a feeling that country life is somehow more real, more genuine than the artificial life of towns. And partly it may be the feeling that, while towns are built exclusively for the benefit of humans, in the country other forms of life, both plant and animal, that are not of immediate benefit to man are allowed to exist alongside him.

All of this has its reflection in religion; for our religion is not a scientific explanation of the origin, nature and purpose of human life but rather an expression of our attitude towards life in general. Social, town-dwelling man has thus built himself a social, urban religion. Christianity is an urban religion. It is built as a town is built exclusively for the benefit of man. It is surrounded by a wall which, like a town wall, serves the double purpose of both keeping out and keeping in. Like the citizens of any large and prosperous town, Christians are rightly proud of their religion, consider all other religions inferior and see it as their duty to bring more and more people within the ever-expanding walls of Christendom. Yet not all people are gregarious, and not all people like the urban, man-centred, bricks-and-mortar, artificial world they find there. And just as it is now possible for those who like it to enjoy rural life without totally forgoing all the benefits of urban life, so it is now possible to live outside Christianity without forgoing all that Christianity has to offer. The city gates, once so vigilantly guarded, now stand open and those who wish may pass to and fro without question. And just as I, though born a Londoner, have passed through the city gates to become a countryman, so, though given a Christian education, I have passed through the gates of Christianity to find what – if I had to give it a name – I would call the rural religion of Pantheism. If the Christian vision of God is of a man-centred God, the God of Love, mine is of a God who looks with equal favour on all forms of life and whom perhaps I could therefore call the God of Beauty.

Are these two forms of God incompatible? Can the Christian claim that he is right and I am therefore wrong? Most certainly not. For though each of us, singly or in groups, may search for and find the truth, it can never be the whole truth. And though the Christian may say – and very properly say – that God is like this and like this, he must remember that what he is describing is not the God who created the universe but his own particular vision of that God.

In the year 1504 the wife of Francesco Zanobi sat for her portrait. No doubt even in that particular year she found time to do other things; and certainly in the years before and after there was much else she did. Yet because the portrait was so good, it was carefully preserved; and because a king of France fell in love with it, it ended up in the Louvre; and because it is still greatly admired, copies of it have been distributed throughout the world. And so the lady whom Leonardo da Vinci painted nearly five hundred years ago is familiar to millions as 'the Mona Lisa', while the little girl, also called Mona Lisa, who ran through the streets of Florence is quite unknown to us. So familiar is the picture, so many copies of it have we seen, that, if asked, we would say without hesitation that the original is still to be found at the Louvre. We forget that the original Mona Lisa was a human being of whom Leonardo gave us only a single glimpse.

In exactly the same way the Bible gives us a glimpse of God, a glimpse that all too readily we mistake for the reality. Just possibly someone might yet disinter a sketch, inexpertly drawn, feeble and faded, but which beyond dispute showed Mona Lisa as a young girl. Such a portrait would never pretend to challenge Leonardo's, but it would undoubtedly add something to our knowledge of the woman he painted. In the same way our differing views of God, whether those of the great religions of the world or of individuals, are not necessarily in competition with each other and may well add to our total understanding of his world. So the Christian should never be afraid (as alas he so often is) to look at a portrait of God that is not Christ's. Nor should he think that by accepting that there may be some truth in this portrait he is in some way being disloyal to Christ's portrait. I say this because I am now going to argue that, two thousand years after that famous portrait was given to us, the time has come when we should, indeed must, attempt another. Whether the world can today produce an artist to match the genius of Christ I do not know, but without such a portrait I doubt if the world can survive.

What threatens our survival? Most people would answer, 'Nuclear war.' Others might say, 'An accidental nuclear disaster.' But there is a third and potentially much greater threat, and it is paradoxically a threat that arises from our very success in combating the lesser threats to human existence. It is as if we are playing a game of snakes and ladders and, having avoided most of the snakes and climbed most of the ladders, we are now within a throw of the top. A single ladder lies ahead of us. But, alas, if we land there, it will carry us not to the top but over the top and we will fall to our death. Less perilous, therefore, are those two snakes that also await us. For a series of nuclear explosions, whether intentional or accidental, and however devastating, would be unlikely to render the entire world uninhabitable. They would send us way back to the bottom of the board, but at least we could start the slow climb again. Best of all, however, if we can manage it, is the throw that avoids all three hazards, takes us to the top, and allows us to stay there.

If you want to understand how the world works, build yourself a garden pond and then, before you fill it up with tap water and throw in half a dozen goldfish and a sprinkling of bread crumbs, acquire a book that tells you how to do the job properly. The book I am studying at the moment (for I am just about to build a pond) has sixteen pages of excellent reading of which the most important are the two devoted to pond ecology.

And so I have learned that the plants and animals inhabiting a pond are not a random collection of species each living an isolated existence but form an interdependent community. Their source of energy is the sun. The sun provides the energy that nourishes (for example) the starwort that in turn feeds the wandering pond snails that in turn feed the leeches. This is called a 'food chain'. Another food chain links microscopic algae to water fleas, water fleas to sticklebacks, sticklebacks to the larvae of the great diving beetle. And there are many others. These chains are not separate but are frequently linked to each other and thus form a 'food web'. It is possible with an understanding of all this and over a period of time to stock one's pond with a range of living creatures forming a food web that will remain in balance without any further interference from outside except the supply of solar energy. The pondmaker can then sit back and admire his creation and see that it is good.

Thus did the Great Pondmaker create the world. He may well have had a special affection for his supreme creation, man, just as every little pondmaker has a special affection for his goldfish. But the goldfish are part of the total web and if they destroy any other part they risk destroying themselves.

The web, I said, must remain in balance. Every species has within itself two great impulses, the impulse to survive and the impulse to reproduce. Thus every link in the web presses outwards against neighbouring links and is held in check by these links pressing inwards. When the opposing forces are equal an equilibrium is established. This equilibrium is a stable one. That is to say, although a small disturbance – a particularly cold winter or dry summer – will upset the balance, a return to normal conditions will see a return to normal populations. If conditions remain altered, then a new point of balance is established. Sometimes, however, something goes wrong. The restraining forces so essential to the balance collapse like a defeated army and there is a population explosion. The food that once nourished the species is totally consumed and the species then starves to death. This is what happens when the over-successful parasite kills off its host. This is what could happen to over-successful man, and it is, I believe, the greatest threat to our survival on earth. If the world ends, it will end not with a bang but with a long-drawn-out groan.

I wrote in an earlier chapter that warfare, which had powered mankind for countless thousands of years, driving him from success to success, was now his enemy. I was there referring to warfare between humans. I might with equal truth have been referring to warfare against non-humans. All was well when the battle was evenly poised. But today we have nature on the run, in full scale retreat. Today we are on the edge of total victory – and total defeat.

Once again Rational Man sees the danger and shouts his warning. Once again Emotional Man shuts his eyes and closes his ears. Surely what was true yesterday must remain true today.

No.

The philosophy of life that western man has embraced and which has taken him to the top, lord, very nearly, of the entire world, now threatens him with extinction.

It was all right once to burn all the wood we needed: there was plenty more. It was all right once to dig for coal when the wood ran out: there was any amount of coal. It was all right once to drill for oil when yet more fuel was required: the supply of oil seemed inexhaustible. But it is not all right to consume anything at a faster rate than it can replace itself when stocks have become dangerously low. Equally it was all right once to grab for our own needs regardless of the needs of other species when so much of the world remained theirs. And it was all right once to allow the human population to expand as fast as it wanted to when the forces limiting expansion were still so great. The ladders helped us on our long climb and the snakes merely slowed down our progress to a respectable rate. But what was once right is right no longer.

This is something which the scientists tell us and which we accept as true – though naturally we would rather not agree with them that the danger is as pressing as they claim. Naturally we would prefer not to change our habits until we are compelled to. And naturally in a world beset with more immediate problems the problem of the conservation of the environment must take second place. It is surely more important that we grow potatoes to feed starving humans than starving Colorado beetles. You can't really expect farmers to fight their battle against weeds, pests and diseases with, as it were, one hand tied voluntarily behind their backs. Isn't it at least to our credit that we have made a start? We protect wild birds. We prevent cruelty to animals. We save the whale. We have nature reserves and wild life parks. We have an International Union for Conservation of Nature and Natural Resources and a World Wild Life Fund. Isn't this enough to be going on with?

No.

This is a problem that cannot be solved by the scientist alone; for it is not only a rational problem. It is an emotional problem too. Scientists can convince our heads. But that is not enough. We must feel the truth in our hearts as well. Only when both voices, reason and emotion, give us the same advice will we accept it, freely, happily and without hesitation. And so the scientist must be joined by the artist and the priest. Particularly the priest.

What exactly is the role of the priest in human society? There was a time, many centuries ago, when the priest was also the scientist, the wise man who knew all there was to be known. It is only in the last few hundred years that science and the church parted company; and to some it may have seemed that when they did so the scientist made off with the lion's share of the treasure of human knowledge. It was Macmurray's argument, and it is mine too, that the priest ought not to see himself as a sort of failed scientist, still clinging to those fragments of scientific truth that his rival left behind. Nor when, more recently still, he lost political power should he see himself as a failed politician. Religion is concerned with men's hearts, not their heads. It offers the heart what the heart cries out for, food for the heart, which may be good food or bad and which can only be judged by its effect on the body. The food that is best for the growing man is not the food that was best for the young child. The food that suits the Asiatic does not equally suit the European. The food that nourished our forefathers is not so nourishing today. Christianity spread westwards rather than eastwards because it offered a philosophy of life perfectly in tune with Europe's aspirations at that time. European man was set to dominate the world. Christianity urged him on. Carrying those twin emblems, the flag and the cross, he moved westwards into the Americas, southwards into Africa and Australia and eastwards into India, subjecting and converting, exploiting, taming, civilizing and killing. And wherever he went he unknowingly upset the balance of nature's forces. He saw hunger and sickness. He fed the hungry and he cured the sick, and they showed their gratitude in the inevitable way, by surviving and multiplying and demanding yet more food and medicine. Each problem he solved created another. Faster and faster he had to go. More and more trees had to be felled. More and more land had to be claimed for agriculture. More and more pests had to be destroyed.

Today our politicians still maintain that 'growth' is the answer to all our problems. Of course it will temporarily alleviate our immediate problem, keeping us happy until after the next election. But no one can surely believe that in a finite world the ever-growing needs of an ever-expanding population can be for ever satisfied. There comes a limit, just as there comes a limit to the number and size of the goldfish that can survive in a pond. We are now so close to that limit that at our present rate of progress by the year 2000 the world's population will have increased by almost half, while a third of the world's arable land will have been lost through degradation and half the timber in our tropical forests will have been consumed. If there is hunger in the world today, what will it be like then?

There can be no doubt that if we are to outlive the twenty-first century we must do two things: limit our human population and limit the demands we make on the rest of creation. This, which happens naturally in a well-balanced pond, is something mankind has to do consciously and deliberately, knowing in our hearts as well as our heads that it is the right thing to do.

At present our hearts are unconvinced. And Christianity, so far from yelling 'Halt!' at the top of its voice, is urging us on as if nothing had changed.

Let me give an illustration.

Lord Hailsham in his autobiography, *The Door Wherein I Went*, devotes his first chapters to a robust defence of Christianity. The great difference, he tells us, between Christianity and most other world religions is that Christianity is 'rectilinear' in its belief about human destiny while the others are 'circular'. By this he means that Christians believe that man, after his life in this world, moves on to another world in which he is united with God in immortality; and this he contrasts with the 'circular' theory that man after death returns to this world, reincarnated in a different form. Of the two theories Lord Hailsham prefers the first. 'I do not believe,' he writes, 'that I ever was, or ever can become, a chaffinch.'

Nor do I. But there is more to be considered than just that. For the value of a person's belief in what happens to him after death lies less in its accuracy than in its effect. We cannot produce rational arguments to support our favoured theory; for all argument is based on experience and all experience is limited to life in this world; and when at last we discover the truth about the next world it is too late to tell others. So it must remain a mystery. But we can guess, and what we guess can have its influence. A belief, for example, that our behaviour in this world is rewarded or punished in the next encourages us to behave well. Less obviously, but no less truly, a belief that we are but pilgrims through this world and that Heaven is our goal inclines us to treat what is thus seen as our temporary home rather as the wayside camper treats his camp site: here this evening, gone first thing tomorrow, so throw the rubbish over the hedge.

If on the other hand we believe that this is the only world we have and that on our death we return to it, we are likely to take greater care of it. If in addition we believe that we may possibly be reincarnated as a chaffinch, we are likely to wish to leave the world a place fit not only for humans to live in but chaffinches too. A belief that men can become chaffinches and chaffinches men encourages respect for all forms of life. While a belief that entry into Heaven is restricted to humans implies that chaffinches and the rest are second-class citizens and may be treated as such. In short, whatever were once the merits of the Christian theory of human destiny and however much this theory may still appeal to us, its influence on our lives has now become harmful.

Even more harmful is the Christian attitude to human life itself. How 'right' it once was and how right it still seems to reduce infant mortality. How 'wrong' it once was and how wrong it still seems to many people to interfere with man's natural desire to procreate. Yet these rights and wrongs now threaten our survival. Somehow we must learn to control our urge to over-produce children. If this needs a civil law, then it must be reinforced by a moral law so that we recognize its justice. Similarly we must learn to control our urge to grab for ourselves – for mankind –

what we should be sharing with the other species. And again if this needs a civil law it must be backed by a moral law.

Can Christianity adapt itself to embrace such laws?

If we want a less than thoroughly pessimistic answer we must recall what happened two thousand years ago.

It was plain – indeed it had been plain for a long time – that man's natural, instinctive philosophy of 'each for himself' was a bad one. And so a law had been framed to give the weak some slight protection against the strong. 'Thou shalt not steal,' said the stern voice of authority. This was a start: a list of things that one must not do and a God of Authority threatening retribution if one disobeyed him. But there must have been many living in Palestine at that time who felt that it was not enough, that mankind ought to take the next step forward, that people ought to do what they felt in their hearts to be right rather than refrain from doing what they were told was wrong, that they ought to be moved by love rather than fear, that they ought to be willing to sacrifice what was theirs for the benefit of others and that these others should include enemies as well as friends, foreigners as well as fellow Jews.

It is one thing to see what needs to happen but quite another to cause it to happen.

There are some who say that what did happen was the direct result of an intervention from outside the world, the intervention of Almighty God, who sent down to earth his divine Son. Others (and I am one) prefer a more natural explanation. But all will agree on this: that if Christ had gone among his fellow Jews offering rational arguments in support of a secular philosophy concerning the brotherhood of man, dictating his thoughts to a team of willing scribes until old age claimed him and he died in his bed, then it is unlikely that anyone outside Palestine would ever have heard of him.

He succeeded during his lifetime because he appealed to men's hearts, to their deepest, strongest and noblest emotions, and he reached and stirred these emotions through what was for them the most powerful force in their lives, their religion. 'Love thy neighbour' was God's command, not man's. And he succeeded after his death because he made himself the supreme exemplar of his philosophy of love and self-sacrifice by allowing himself to be put to death for his beliefs. As a scion grows from its stock so did Christianity grow from Judaism and spread throughout the western world.

Thus it happened two thousand years ago; and now the need comes again. We have learned that we must live, not only for ourselves and our families, but for all human beings, whether friends or strangers, and whatever their race. We must now learn to live not only for fellow humans but for all creatures. Just as the God of Authority grew into the God of Love, so now must the God of Love grow into the God of Beauty.

So, while the Christian dreams of the Second Coming and the humanist dreams of Perfect Man, I dream of a new religion, a religion which sees man as the Guardian of the World, the Lord and Protector of all life.

This religion will view the attempts of humans to claim more land for agriculture, to drain more marshes and fell more forests, to build more motorways and airports, more new towns and suburbs, to wrench more minerals from the soil, tip more waste into rivers, turn more peaceful estuaries into marinas – will view such attempts not as something to be opposed at planning enquiries by a handful of individuals calling themselves conservationists and ecologists, but as a crime to be punished by the law and as a sin to be condemned by the new church. I look to the day when man's advance over the surface of the globe, building new colonies for himself, grabbing more food for himself, slaughtering, poisoning, defiling, fouling and trampling into the dust is first halted and then put into reverse; to the day when mankind hands back much of what it has captured, as a victorious but generous nation will hand back to its defeated enemy the territorial conquests of its victory; to the day when our towns and villages are once again small and compact, when fish come again to our rivers and the desert blooms because all men worship the new vision of God.

Such a religion may well require its prophet, its champion, its martyr, its hero and its paragon, because, whether or not we believe or need to believe in the supernatural, our hearts can still be as deeply stirred today as they were stirred two thousand years ago by the life and death of a single human being. Such a religion may well require its legend, its rituals, and its creed, and it will certainly need the assistance of artists and architects, poets and musicians. Such a religion will need its Bible, a Bible in which to the Old Testament and the New Testament already familiar to us has been added a third testament: the Testament of Beauty.

An impossible dream? No, not impossible. For what has happened once can surely happen again.